James Macdonald

Light in Africa

James Macdonald

Light in Africa

ISBN/EAN: 9783744757263

Printed in Europe, USA, Canada, Australia, Japan

Cover: Foto ©Lupo / pixelio.de

More available books at **www.hansebooks.com**

LIGHT IN AFRICA.

BY THE

REV. JAMES MACDONALD.

London:
HODDER AND STOUGHTON,
27, PATERNOSTER ROW.

MDCCCXC.

Printed by Lorimer & Gillies, 31 St. Andrew Square, Edinburgh.

PREFACE.

The following pages are a partial record of personal experience. The facts selected may not be the most interesting that might have been published, but they are those which seemed to give the most accurate idea of life and work in the African mission field.

The chapter on customs and habits is no more than an outline of a subject of engrossing interest. It is only when native life is fully understood that Europeans can enter into sympathy with those who are in a state of barbarism, and realise the value of christianity and civilisation to them. True it is, that a certain class of men persist in the infatuation that the raw native is superior to the trained and educated one. It may be more easy for some men to get along with an untutored African ; he takes more kindly to a kick than the educated man does, but the latter commands the higher wage in the labour market, and employers are a wise people.

Some readers may feel disappointed that greater prominence has not been given to the work of preaching and individual conversions from heathenism. These are subjects of profound interest to the missionary, but they are dealt with in most missionary books, and it was thought better to take a more general view of the work as bringing more clearly before the mind the nature of the influence exerted by missions on the community.

Should anything written deepen the public interest in missions and the welfare of African peoples, the writer's object will be fully served.

The chapter on the habits of animals and insects is added in the hope that it may be of some little interest to lovers of nature, who have not had the advantage of a scientific education.

REAY FREE MANSE,
October, 1890.

CONTENTS.

CHAPTER I.
SOUTHERN AFRICA, . . . 1

CHAPTER II.
LOVEDALE AND ITS WORK, ... 12

CHAPTER III.
PHASES OF MISSION WORK, . . . 25

CHAPTER IV.
THE TRANSKEI—BLYTHSWOOD, . . 44

CHAPTER V.
PEACE—DIPLOMACY—WAR, 56

CHAPTER VI.
FRESH TROUBLES—BURNED HOMESTEADS AND RUINED MISSIONS, . . 86

CHAPTER VII.

JOURNEYS AND EXTENDED MISSIONARY OPERATIONS, . 98

CHAPTER VIII.

EAST GRIQUALAND — NEW MISSIONS — NOVEL EXPERIENCES, ... 121

CHAPTER IX.

THE NATIVE AFRICANS—THEIR CUSTOMS AND HABITS, . 148

CHAPTER X.

STRAY STUDIES OF ANIMAL LIFE, 233

CHAPTER XI.

CLIMATE AND TEMPERATURE, . . 259

I.

SOUTHERN AFRICA.

SO much has recently been written about Africa that any thing connected with the quiet of Mission life must appear modest and uninteresting, when compared with stirring events and great discoveries in other parts of the Continent. But to all who take an interest in the moral and spiritual progress of the human race, everything calculated to throw light on the problems that have to be grappled with is welcome. The experience of the past can be compared with the facts of the present, and new questions can, with confidence, be approached in the light of such experience.

The twelve years I spent in Southern Africa afforded exceptional opportunities for observing African natives, and studying their customs and habits of life, both under conditions of profound peace, and during famine and war. A brief record of my experiences, in different localities, may not be devoid of interest to those whose attention has been turned to the complex problems which await solution throughout the African Continent. It is my intention, in the following pages, to confine myself to what I have seen and heard, and if by so doing, I seem to give an undue prominence to Scotch Missions, it is not because I undervalue the work of others, for the Missionary Societies, one and all, are doing a noble work in the cause of human progress and enlightenment.

On the 21st of July, 1875, I left London on my way to the Mission field, and after something over three weeks of lazy steaming, arrived at Cape Town. It was my first long sea voyage, and after paying the usual tribute to Neptune, I enjoyed it intensely. It was a new experience; and both in the forecastle and among the passengers I soon made many friends. Through the kindness of the late Rev. P. Hope I had an excellent assortment of books and periodicals for distribution among the crew. That these were thoroughly appreciated I knew, from many of the men having come to me oftener than once to ask for a fresh supply. Then the Sunday services had a novelty about them quite foreign to our ordinary church service. It was altogether a charming experience; one which can only belong to a first voyage, and of which I have a most vivid recollection even at this distance of time.

At Cape Town I was met by the late Professor Noble, of the South African College, who showed me all manner of kindness during my brief stay in the Colonial capital. Of the few days at my disposal, one was spent at Stellenbosch, which is the chief educational centre in the Colony. Here the Dutch Reformed Church has a well-equipped Gymnasium and a Theological Hall. There is also the Victoria College, with an efficient staff of Professors, who deliver lectures on science, especially Chemistry and Natural Philosophy, Mathematics, Mental and Moral Philosophy, and Classics. The curriculum is very complete, and the education given is quite equal to our Scotch University undergraduate course. Two large boarding establishments, one under American management, the other under the auspices of the Rhenish Mission, represent, not at all amiss, our boarding-schools for young ladies in the home country. Whatever may be the condition of the up-country Dutch Boers, those living near the centres of population are fully alive to the necessity of a good sound education for all classes of the community.

What interested me most about Cape Town was the number of nationalities represented there. There is not a nation under heaven whose citizens do not dwell under the shade of Table Mountain; from busy, bustling John Bull, to the contemplative disciple of the Prophet, who has there made a home for himself and his religion, and who, with flowing robe and slow measured pace, perambulates the busy streets between his stated hours of prayer. The keen Yankee from beyond the Rocky Mountains rubs shoulders with the swarthy South American, who has just a trace of the Moor in his features, and a stream of Spanish blood in his veins. The latter does a "big thing" in mules, while the former is chiefly interested in sealing expeditions to the cold waters of the south. Turks and Arabians drive a brisk trade in imported Angora goats, and Greeks man coasting vessels and Indian traders. The Chinaman flits about the guest's chair in hotels, and the Malay conducts the fruit trade of the community. Our more stolid Dutchman, once absolute ruler at the Cape, does not take kindly to this busy cosmopolitan life, and has practically retired to the country, where his cattle, his pipe, coffee, and occasional "soopie," afford him employment, solace, and hilarity, more in the direction of his tastes and inclinations. Certain modes of life develop corresponding habits, and it is not to be wondered at that men roaming over illimitable plains tending cattle, and carrying their whole possessions in a single waggon, should have acquired habits of indolence which it will take generations to eradicate.

The early Dutch Boers occupied runs of considerable extent, reaching usually to many miles in every direction, and yet neighbours were often at feud about boundaries. There were no surveyors nor surveyor's implements in the country, and the "official pacer," or *Veldt wagt meester*, could take an extra long step when measuring for a friend or favourite. The Boer himself, absolute master of these wide domains, free alike from the calls of the tax-gatherer and the conscript, usually left his flocks and herds to the care of his Hottentot slaves. His pipe seldom quitted his mouth except when he slept, or eat his three daily meals of mutton sodden in fat. The good lady of the house, equally disdainful of toil, remained almost as immovable as her lord. She usually sat in a chair, having before her a table always well supplied with hot coffee, while her daughters sat with folded arms, resembling articles of furniture more than ordinary human beings. The sons spent their time hunting or breaking in young horses. No diversion ever broke the monotony of this existence. Newspapers never penetrated the vast solitudes of the Karoo. Ignorance, stupidity, and prejudice found here a rich soil in which to thrive, and the fruits of it are to-day manifest in the condition of the northern border of the Transvaal Republic. With all this ignorance and practically nomadic mode of life hospitality hardly knew any bounds. The stranger opened the door, shook hands with the master, kissed the mistress, and with a nod to the younger members took his seat and was welcome. Things are greatly changed now-a-days; there is hardly a village or hamlet in the Colony without a good school, and many of the Dutch colonists are among the most refined people in the country. Slavery has given place to free labour, and a degree of energy has been infused into the population that is rapidly changing the whole social life of the people. Still, the quiet pastoral life of the past has a charm for many, and men of education and wealth are still found tending huge droves of cattle and flocks of sheep, with no other source of pleasure and amusement than is afforded by the lowing and bleating round the fold when the herds return with their charge for the night.

My purpose is not, however, to write the "Story of an African Farm," so we must hurry on to Kaffraria, where I was for the first time introduced to the savage life of the Bantu tribes.

On the 23rd of August I landed at Algoa Bay, and after spending three most enjoyable days there I proceeded on my journey inland. The railway system of the colony was at this time in its infancy, and the journey to Graham's Town was still performed either by coach or in the old-fashioned bullock waggon. I found it more convenient as well as expeditious to travel by coach, and at 4 A.M. on the 26th I took my seat in one of Cobb's famous vehicles. It was advertised to arrive at Graham's Town, a distance of about 100 miles, at 8 P.M., and to stop half-an-hour at convenient hostelries for breakfast and dinner. But, as often happens, promise is one thing, performance is quite another. As we proceeded one accident succeeded another with almost alarming frequency. First a recalcitrant team of horses refused to budge a step. At the next stage the team which should have been ready waiting for us had been turned out to graze, and the coach had to wait until they were driven home and caught. Finally an axletree became heated, and took a long time to cool and re-adjust. These and sundry smaller accidents of broken belts delayed us long into the night, and instead of rattling up the High Street of Graham's Town at dusk to the music of the merry sounding horn, we came lumbering slowly into town just before dawn.

But any reference to African travelling would be incomplete without an account of the vehicles in use at the time of which I write. A "Cobb's Coach" is built somewhat on the principle of an American waggon, but is suspended on strong leathern straps instead of being set on springs in the usual fashion. This gives it a swinging motion, which at first feels very disagreeable, but is found to lessen the severe jolting to which spring vehicles are liable on uneven roads. It is covered with a light canvas roof to give protection from sun and rain. There is no raised box for the driver. He sits in a corner of the front seat, "under his cattles' tails," and his team consists of six or eight horses, yoked two and two.

When the mails and passengers' baggage have been strapped securely on the rear platform, the driver climbs into his corner, and after he has settled himself tests the length of the coupling pieces between the respective pairs of horses; makes sure that his "long thong" is in good order, and that sundry other articles are at hand. Having satisfied himself on these points he motions the strapper to stand aside, and suddenly yells the word *yek*, and away scamper his ragged-looking team at full gallop. This functionary is usually an ancient Hottentot, in yet more ancient corduroys. And reader, if you ever travel by a " Cobb's " on the box-seat, in a blazing African sun, you will then realise how old corduroys, old Hottentots, and stale brandy smell.

A day on the road in Africa is a trying ordeal. The rough roads jolt one from side to side in the most provoking manner, and as the day wears on towards afternoon the irritation caused by dust, flies, and heat is almost intolerable. There is besides that odoriferous emanation from the corduroys—like a true Scotchman, I seem to *feel* that smell now. The most hardened globe-trotter could not endure it patiently.

Of Graham's Town I had heard much. Some described it as a perfect paradise, while others spoke of it as the most utterly forsaken borough in the Colony. Both accounts had an element of truth. The glory of brass bands and military parades had long departed, and what was once a large garrison town is now a quiet rural centre of trade. What it has lost in stir and bustle it has gained in beauty and solid comfort. A writer, in 1830, described Graham's Town as " a large, ugly, ill-built, straggling place, containing a strange mixture of lounging officers, idle tradesmen, drunken soldiers, and still more drunken settlers." I found it in 1875 a well-built, well-paved, and well-lighted town, made the ideal of rural beauty by the rows of magnificent trees growing on the edge of the footpaths. Every thoroughfare is an avenue of oaks or blackwoods, and every garden is filled with choicest fruit trees. The situation is, besides, most romantic, being in a deep hollow surrounded by green and grassy hills, and these separated by deep narrow gorges, overhung by thickly wooded banks and frowning precipices.

My brief visit was exceedingly pleasant, and when a few months thereafter I revisited the city to supply, temporarily, the pulpit of the Presbyterian Church, my early impressions were confirmed. Instead of drunken settlers, I met with unbounded hospitality from a refined and educated community, almost every one of whom was a son or daughter of the much maligned settlers of 1820. The journey from Graham's Town to Beaufort was performed by coach, and differed in no essential from that already described, only that we arrived at the latter place half-an-hour before the advertised time. At Beaufort I was met by William Koyi, who was sent from Lovedale with a private vehicle to drive me to my destination, which I reached before midnight, on the 29th of August.

As William Koyi was one of the most remarkable men of his own nation, and a striking illustration of successful missionary work, I shall here give a brief history of his career. What follows is partly from my own recollection and notes, partly from "Lovedale Past and Present," a publication which should be in the hands of all interested in heathen lands.

William Koyi was a pure Gaika Kaffir, and was born at Thomas River in the year 1846. During the cattle killing mania in 1857, and when only eleven years of age, he left his home as an alternative to starvation, and went to seek employment among the Dutch farmers in the Colony. He was employed by a man who gave him half-a-crown a month as leader of his waggon oxen, and at this work he continued for some years. After leaving his Dutch employer he got a situation in a wool-washing establishment at Utenhage, and rose to the position of overseer. His next employment was with Messrs. A. C. Stewart, of Port-Elizabeth, where he remained for five years. He had never been to school, and now for the first time he began to feel the need of education, and set about learning to read Kaffir. About 1869 he was converted to Christianity, and admitted a member of the Wesleyan Church. His desire for education now became a passion, but he had neither leisure nor opportunity to prosecute his studies. He one day picked up a stray leaf of the *Isigidimi Sama-Xosa*, and from it first learned something about Lovedale. On making inquiries about the place of which he had read, he found it was over 150 miles away. This did not daunt him. He resigned his situation and made his way to the Institution. He attended the ordinary school course at Lovedale, and during his stay there was active, willing, and trustworthy. He earned the respect of all, and the Europeans with whom he came into contact regarded him as a friend rather than as an ordinary pupil. As at the wool wash, so at Lovedale, he soon rose to a position of trust and responsibility. Since childhood he had neither known father nor mother, and came to look upon Lovedale as his home. During my acquaintance with William at Lovedale I came to regard him as a man of sterling character, who was always striving to rise to a higher and nobler life, who keenly felt the need of a higher spiritual life. He always had before him a high moral ideal.

In 1876, he volunteered to go to Livingstonia, and while others offered as evangelists or teachers, William expressed his willingness to go as a " hewer of wood and drawer of water." For ten years he steadily laboured there, coming only once to re-visit his home and friends at Lovedale. On that occasion he married a daughter of the late Rev. A. Van Rooyen, and returned full of hope to his work in Central Africa. He was not destined to return home again, but, like many other devoted men of God, to lay down his life when in the full tide of useful labour.

II.

LOVEDALE AND ITS WORK.

WILLIAM and I reached Lovedale shortly after 11 P.M., where I was most cordially welcomed by Mrs. Stewart and several members of the Mission staff who waited my arrival. Mrs. Stewart I found a bright, active happy lady, whose hospitality was proverbial, and who to myself showed, during my stay at Lovedale, a degree of kindness which quite exceeded anything I had a right to expect; and this, too, at very considerable inconvenience and trouble. I felt at home with her from the first hour.

On the Sunday after my arrival I accompanied the Rev. Mr. Moir to the station of Macfarlane, where he was to dispense the Eucharist in the native church. It was the first time I had met a congregation of native African worshippers gathered to engage in solemn service to God. The sensation was peculiar. There was the crowd of flat copper-coloured and far from comely faces, relieved only by their bright twinkling eyes. There were the gorgeous coloured pyramids of handkerchiefs with which the women adorned their heads. Their black babies, *in puris naturalibus*, sprawled about the floor beside their mothers, or made short pilgrimages, on all fours, to the reader's desk as if to see what the noise was about. Away at the back, and seated chiefly on the floor, was a crowd of men and women in terra-cotta blankets and redolent of grease and red clay. These were heathens who had come to church out of curiosity, or as a variety to sitting gossiping by the beer pots, and who from choice rather than necessity generally sit on the floor when attending a place of worship, or, indeed, on any occasion when there is a crowd. When the service began, and a Kaffir hymn was sung to the well known tune " Balerma," I fairly stared, and for a moment felt as if almost bewildered. The sermon was spoken in English and translated sentence by sentence into Kaffir. It was simple, plain, practical, and pointed. The firing was low, very low, but one felt that the aim was true, and the close attention given by both Christians and heathens showed clearly that the simple direct style of address adopted was well suited to their circumstances and capacity. I have no record of the number who communicated, but I remember that they were a goodly company, and that the table service, in which I took part, was solemn and impressive.

It is impossible to meet a congregation of Christian worshippers, for the first time, in heathen lands without very mixed feelings. There is the difference of race and of language; of habits and customs; of thought and feeling. And there is again the sense of the common brotherhood of the great human family; that of one blood are all the nations of the earth, savage and civilised, and that all the different types are but so many departures, upwards and downwards, from a common ancestor. But deeper than all these general considerations is the feeling of the believer's oneness in Christ Jesus, and that men of European and African origin, sitting there and partaking of the symbols of the broken body and shed blood of the Incarnate One, are brethren in Christ, and partakers of the same hope. The thoughts passing through one's mind on such occasions are too deep for words; too sacred for utterance, and explain it by what philosophy we will, it is during such moments life's resolves are made and life's battles fought and won.

On the 8th of September, Dr. Stewart, who since my arrival had been absent in the Transkei, on Blythswood business, returned. He was very tired and haggard-looking, and to me he seemed in rather a sorry plight. Twelve miles from Lovedale, while descending a steep hill in the dark, one of his "spider" wheels came off, and he had first to go in search of native huts where he could borrow saddles for himself and his groom, which could only be got after much negotiation. Having got the saddles their next care was to get the "spider" out of the way of other vehicles, and leave it there until the following morning. I viewed such an accident in a serious light, but the Doctor seemed to regard it as a very ordinary incident of African travel, and merely remarked on the awkwardness of having to send men to bring home the disabled vehicle on the following day. He observed my stare of astonishment, and, with a merry twinkle in his eyes, said, "Before you are three years in this country you will learn to think as little of such things as I do." He then proceeded to explain that any one who travels in Africa must make up his mind to have to go farther than he expects at the start, to pay out more money than he has calculated, and to take more time than seems necessary for the journey. The philosophical application of these three excellent rules I often found of great value in after years, as will every one who attempts to accomplish anything in the Dark Continent.

The Lovedale Mission staff at this time consisted of Dr. Stewart, who is a man of high intellectual attainments and nervous temperament, but apt at times to be fretful and impatient. His sympathy with every form of suffering; his kindness and hospitality; his devotion to the cause of Africa, and the truly catholic spirit of his deep though unostentatious piety have endeared him to all who know him and learn to understand and appreciate the excellences of his character. His clear grasp of all matters connected with the great institution of which he is the head, as well as of general missionary work in the country, has enabled him to build up from small beginnings a fabric which is unique of its kind.

The Rev. Mr. Moir is, again, the antithesis of Dr.

Stewart, and has from the first filled a place in the Institution and Mission which is peculiarly his own. He has done, and is doing now, good solid and abiding work. The other teachers were Messrs. Smith, Theal, Bennie, and Dorrington. Mr. Smith made Africa the scene of his life's work, and as a Professor at Lovedale impressed the mark of his own earnest character on many youths both European and African.

Mr. Theal I liked from the first. A real good-hearted, hard-working American was he. He was, moreover, a man with a grievance. He could no more live without one than he could without breathing. Since he left Lovedale, during the war of 1877, he has had a successful career as a native administrator and as an author, but he still clings to a grievance, though it is neither allowed to interfere with the efficient discharge of his duties nor with his own comfort in life. I like the man with a good stock grievance. It gives point and zest to life and social intercourse, and I like Mr. Theal none the less, but rather the better, because whenever we meet, I always find him with a fresh cause of grumble.

The Girls' School was under the care of the Misses MacRitchie and Kayser. The latter married a prosperous farmer from Natal, and is, I have no doubt, busy and contented among her "bairns" and poultry. The former left Lovedale for the United Presbyterian Mission School at Emgwali. She is now conducting a private native school in King William's Town.

On the 13th of September I began regular work in the Institution; but I must here make a digression to say a few words about the origin and development of Lovedale. Few of those who are now the warmest and heartiest supporters of African Missions are familiar with the early history of the movement, nor is it possible, in the fragmentary sketch I am about to give, to touch upon the many trials, difficulties, disappointments, and losses of the early missionaries. Solitary graves, surrounded by a wall of rough uneven stones and a few trees, speak of bereavement and sorrow. The old foundations of buildings, still growing moss and lichen, recall the days of war and burning and much woe. Rows of cactus and aloe, now grown into a dense jungle, bear witness to the taste and industry of those pioneers of Christian civilisation, while the stately edifice of the native church remains as a monument of their faith and perseverance. After a great deal of negotiation, the site of Lovedale was chosen. A small grant of land was given to the Mission by the Government of the day, and operations commenced on a very modest scale. For a time the work was confined to preaching to the surrounding heathens, and doing something towards the establishment of a small day school. Buttons and beads were the currency, and these were at times used to bring the children to school. From such small beginnings did that Institution, which is now the pride of the mother Church, as well as one of the "lions" of South Africa, take its origin. The men who paid in buttons and beads for cutting down the dense jungle before they began to build, in 1837, could hardly foresee that, in 1882, the sum of £2000 would be paid by native Africans, as fees for education at Lovedale alone, and that many other schools throughout the country would be, in great part, supported by native contributions.

As time went on, the question of more advanced education for the missionaries' children, and such natives as might desire it, arose, and in 1841, the Rev. W. Govan opened the place as a boarding establishment, with eleven natives and nine Europeans. Three times since then the work has been interrupted by war, and on one occasion the class rooms and dormitories were turned into accommodation for soldiers and military stores.

About 1856, industrial training, in a number of branches of trade, was added to the work of the Institution. This was the result of a visit paid to the place by Sir George Grey, who was then Governor at the Cape. He took a deep interest in the welfare of the native races, and, being much pleased with the work at Lovedale, gave £3000 from the Civil Lists to help in the erection of the necessary buildings and the purchase of plant. This appears a large sum of money, and so it is, but it does not cover more than a tenth of what has been spent on buildings at Lovedale. Not less than £30,000 has, from first to last, been spent there, exclusive of the ordinary current yearly expenditure for working and maintenance.

Between the date of Sir George Grey's visit in 1856 and 1871, when for the first time fees were charged, the attendance and the results fluctuated considerably. From 1870 to 1877 the growth was steady and sustained in all departments, but in the latter year war brought reverses, and the native fees fell from £1665 in 1876, to £636 in 1878. The reverses suffered during the war were speedily made up, and the Institution, in three years, regained more than it had lost. In 1882, no less a sum than £2000 was paid as fees by natives, and that at a spot where, less than sixty years before, naked savages laboured clearing a space for the building, at six buttons per day. To the expenditure on buildings and maintenance, falls to be added the salary of missionaries, and the sums expended by the Church in various ways, as well as several large donations and legacies, making the yearly expenditure something between three and four thousand pounds sterling.

It is this large expenditure which makes the public, or a certain section of it, so jealous of missionary institutions and Christian colleges; and if it can be shown that the money is well spent, and that adequate results are obtained, all the recent criticism of missionaries and their methods must be set aside as merely the expression of ill-formed opinion, Canon Taylor notwithstanding.

The objects aimed at in what we may call higher missionary education, may be briefly stated thus:—

to give stability and permanency to results obtained by other agencies.

But it is often said that the native makes no use of such education and training, and that he is as well, or even better without it. This objection hardly deserves serious reply. If education and careful moral training can convert a raw African lad into such a sterling man as William Koyi became, and as many others who are leading useful lives as ministers, teachers, clerks, storemen, and mechanics have become, it carries the evidence of its own success in its practical results.

I find from "Lovedale Past and Present," a book recently issued from the Lovedale Mission Press, that out of 2458, whose names have at one time or another been on the books of the Institution, that there were then 16 ministers, 20 evangelists, 376 teachers, 6 lawyers, 3 journalists, 1213 in various employments, 214 were casual labourers or living at their homes, while only 15 had relapsed into open and avowed heathenism, 246 were still at Lovedale. From this brief summary it does not appear as if missionary education were devoid of results. The goodly army of 376 teachers is surely doing something to let light and sweetness into the dark places of the earth, and the artisans must do something towards improving the bee-hive dwelling and solving that old riddle how to square the circle. The small number of fifteen relapsed into open heathenism will be a surprise to many friends of Missions, who may have been led, through inaccurate statements, to regard a loss of fifty per cent. or even more as quite possible from this cause alone. For it is the case that this going back to a former life has been supposed to be the standing reproach of missionary work, and an irrefutable proof of its want of stability and permanency. It is referred to in books of travel where the writer has picked up a few untested opinions and transferred them to his journal, with a number of moral reflections, to reappear in the pages of his book with all the authority of an admitted truth. Now this popular error is due to two causes. It is supposed on the one hand that the number who do actually relapse is greater than it really is, and on the other, that whoever wears European clothing and associates less or more with Christian men is himself converted to Christianity.

But every native who wears a suit of clothes and comes to church as a variety to beer drinking and discussing the "points" of oxen, or as a new form of mild excitement, is not a Christian, nor does he profess to be one. It is true we often have to lament over relapses into the old heathenism, but so had St. Paul before us, and yet his work was of a permanent character. It remains, after more than eighteen centuries of trial, a monument of the power and efficacy of that Gospel which, beginning from Galilee, has spread over a vast portion of the world, and the work of modern missions is nothing else than the continuance and development of that which was then begun. In so far as the work is consistent with the spirit of Christianity, neither popular works of fiction nor the shallow and hastily formed opinions of travellers can affect its stability or the place which it has always held in public Christian sympathy.

But it is often urged that the raw native in his heathen simplicity is preferable to the educated native, and that if to this simplicity we were to add "the preaching of the simple Gospel"—whatever that may mean, for on the point our detractors are not at all agreed—his condition would become an ideal one. This depends on our conception of excellency. The raw Kaffir has few thoughts except for his cattle and the spirits which haunt him. He has a dozen different words for cows or oxen with peculiar daplings of skin where the European has but one. But when the question is not regarding the herding of cows and the tending of calves, the supposed advantages of the native in his savage simplicity disappears. When the question is regarding work requiring skill and thought, from the construction of the simplest square box upwards, the advantage is all on the side of the educated man, be he native African or European. By the process of education, his intelligence has been sharpened and faculties awakened that were entirely dormant before his instruction was commenced. Such skill as he has acquired in the use of tools he can turn to better account if he has a measure of understanding of what the finished product is to be, and the more perfect his comprehension of processes in manufacture, the more valuable will be his work.

Then as regards the number passing through the classes at Lovedale, though comparatively small when the whole population is taken into account, it is such as cannnt fail to make an impression upon their countrymen in time. There is a small number of educated men, which is steadily increasing, who are possessed of acquirements and knowledge of which their fathers did not dream. These, as books and readers increase, will influence the native community, and that in a most powerful manner. There are also those who have acquired mechanical skill, and who can at the far distant family home turn out articles which surprise and delight a whole hamlet, and which the wisest artificers, who jealously kept the secrets of their craft, could not do in the days of the fathers. By such means the whole aspect of African life is being silently but effectually changed.

The new mysterious power which has been introduced into the country, and which finds expression in young men sawing logs into boards and beams, shaping, jointing, and ornamenting these as they are made into articles of daily use ; making shoes out of cow hide and calf skin ; forming garments to fit the person "like a man's skin ; " and producing articles of strange form and for strange uses on the anvil, is slowly but surely laying the foundation of a revolution in the whole domestic life of the people, and such, if wisely guided, will be a benefit and blessing to all. To give direction and colour to such movements we must have educated men, and education founded on Christian principles is unquestionably the most catholic, and that which is best calculated—judging by all human experience—to accomplish the end in view.

Stock thefts and cattle raids have done more to disturb the peace of the frontier, than all other causes combined, and in these the educated native seldom takes part. Whatever individuals may have done, the educated section of the community have not joined their countrymen in time of war, and they have, more than once, been the means of avoiding bloodshed and much woe. This must be traced in large measure to Christian work and influence.

III.

PHASES OF MISSION WORK.

I FIND from my journal that on the 23rd September I was present at an anniversary meeting at Gaga, an out-station under the Lovedale Native Church. Such meetings I attended frequently in after years, and refer to this one, rather to show the crude ideas formed by the novice, when for the first time introduced to new and strange conditions of life, than from any importance attaching to the meeting as such. I transfer the entry as it stands. It is as follows :—

Arrived at the Station (Gaga), I noticed dense volumes of smoke issuing from a small hollow or natural pit close at hand, and proceeded to explore the mystery. There I found a large circle of fires, with huge three-legged pots set in order on them, while round them stood a number of old women. Young men, almost naked, danced about in the smoke attending to the fires, ramming pointed sticks into one pot, pouring grain into a second, and water into a third. Great pieces of beef and mutton were being carried about to and from the pots, and the scene looked as if a showman's monkeys had been let loose, and were playing pranks with the kitchen and larder. Dense bitter smoke rose from fires made of wood almost green, volumes of steam, as from a witch's cauldron, issued from the pots while the women stirred their contents. This and the hubbub of voices gave to the scene something of the appearance in actual fact and grim reality, of the pagan descriptions of a place that need not be named. And yet all the preparation was for the purpose of a religious meeting!

Presently the bell began to ring, that is to say, a very old barefooted man began to beat with a stone a disused cart-wheel tire, suspended between two undressed poles of wood, and to the sound of this uncertain music we marched into the church. This was a small but fairly comfortable building, floored with hard earth, and fitted with strong serviceable benches. The religious part of the service was conducted by the Rev. Mr. Moir, who preached a long discourse, and afterwards spoke at some length about various practical matters connected with the station, including its buildings, school, and general organisation. At the close he read the financial statement, and announced that the collection for the day amounted to £8, 2s., besides what had been provided for the feast to which we were about to repair. During all this time the congregation sat patiently and listened with marvellous attention, considering the interest they had in the progress of the proceedings in the pit outside. But no sooner was the benediction pronounced and the service closed, than the whole congregation made a rush for the pots, and sitting down in companies prepared for the more serious business of the day. Few, if any, had partaken of breakfast, and they settled down to their meal with sharpened appetite if not with sharpened teeth. After the meal was ended, singing and merry-making began, and the day closed to the satisfaction of everybody—much the same as any holiday or dancing party comes to an end.

Such was the impression made on my mind by the first religious anniversary I attended in Africa, and it seems necessary to explain how such a system, so contrary to all our ideas of what a solemn service ought to be, originated. In the early days of Missions, converts were gathered in small groups round the station, and were forbidden from all participation in their national amusements. By sound of bell the whole community were called to morning and evening prayers, and an unwritten Curfew system existed, which effectually prevented any breach of station rules. At weddings, neither music nor dancing were allowed, and David's Psalms, rendered into very indifferent Kaffir verse, took the place of the inspiriting strains of the ancient national music. The natural craving for amusement being suppressed in legitimate directions, found expression in such gatherings as were professedly of a religious nature, till the holding of anniversaries and other periodical gatherings threatened to become a public scandal. Such meetings were frequently prolonged far into the night, and I have known instances in which the feasting and singing was resumed on the following day.

My next visit was to the romantic Mission of Burnshill, where I received a cordial welcome from its energetic missionary, the Rev. D. MacLeod, who was even then suffering from that fell disease which ultimately ended his useful life. Only when he was gone from us did we realise the extent of our loss. His work in Africa was brief—only four years, but in that short time he did much good work, and his last hours were spent within sound of the din of war and bloodshed in the early months of 1878.

From Burnshill I proceeded to Pirie. There I met for the first time the venerable Rev. John Ross, one of the pioneers of Kaffir Missions, and his two sons Bryce and Richard; the former missionary at Pirie, the latter at Cunningham, in the Transkei. Dr. Bryce Ross is a quiet, studious, and thoughtful man, who, in mediæval times, would have made an ideal monk, and would have left behind him monuments of careful industry and learning for the use of coming generations, while Richard is a bustling, busy, practical worker, who, in former days, would have found his true vocation as a knight-errant, redressing wrongs and putting all things to rights in accordance with his conception of the fitness of things. Each in his own way has done a vast amount of good work for the Mission, the former in connection with Bible translation and Kaffir scholarship, the latter in extending the evangelistic side of the work, especially in the Transkei.

While at Lovedale I made the acquaintance of several of the French missionaries in Basutoland. Two of them, The Revs. Messrs. Colliard and Mabille, visited the Institution, and were, while there, the guests of Dr. Stewart, and as I also lived in his house, I saw much of them. What impressed me most about them was the simple unaffected character of their faith and piety. That they had individuality of character, and that Mr. Colliard especially, was a man of intellectual culture no one could fail to observe, but the simplicity of their faith and their trust in Divine guidance seemed a reproof to those who might be inclined to lay stress on methods and careful organisation, to the possible exclusion of other factors and forces, less easily seen and recognised, but none the less real. Since that time Mr. Colliard has displayed some of the highest qualities of the successful traveller and diplomatist in connection with the Mission to the Barosti, while Mr. Mabille has been successful in organising a missionary institution and training school at Maseru, in Basutoland. When organising our own new Missions in East Griqualand from 1882 to 1887, I saw much of the work done by our French brethren, and its character confirmed the early estimate formed of the men.

The 5th of November, 1875, was a day of very peculiar interest in the history of Lovedale. On that day a meeting was held with the native congregation for the purpose of electing a minister, one of their own people, after the Presbyterian fashion of popular election in Scotland. Two young men, trained at Lovedale, had been duly licensed as preachers by the local Presbytery, and the choice lay between them. After the congregation had assembled, the nature of business was minutely explained, but explanation is one thing, comprehension quite another. To all of them the nature of the business was entirely new, and they seemed utterly unable to comprehend it, and only after the doors were locked and the roll of members called over slowly, amidst many interruptions, could the Presbytery ascertain, even approximately, the mind of the meeting and the position of parties. Everything comes to an end, and so at last did the communion roll of the Lovedale church, when it was found that the choice of the majority was the Rev. Pambani Mzimba. The 2nd of December was fixed for his ordination. The congregation was then dismissed, the majority hardly comprehending what it had all been about, so difficult is it to introduce the simplest ideas to the native mind for the first time.

But if this sense of half-dazed surprise and imperfect comprehension had no other effect, it was a good preparation for a large gathering on the day of ordination. Long before the hour of meeting, people began to arrive, many of them from distances of scores of miles, and when at noon the Presbytery repaired to the church, it was filled to suffocation, while several hundreds were unable to gain admission. There was nothing for it but to adjourn to the open air, and assemble under the shade of the blue gum trees. It was there, under the vault of heaven, that the first Free Church Kaffir pastor was ordained to the charge of a congregation of Christian worshippers. The settlement has proved a happy one, and Mr. Mzimba, after fourteen years of work, still holds the hearts and affections of his people. My acquaintance with his work ceased about a year after his ordination, but the continued prosperity of his congregation, and the general esteem in which he is held, is ample evidence that under favourable conditions the native pastor is quite capable of doing the work required in the present state of development in the native Church.

How long it may be before the native pastors can undertake the entire responsibility of church work, without any European guidance, it is difficult to say, but experience clearly proves that too early withdrawal is simply disastrous. Evidence of this is furnished by once prosperous stations that now resemble stranded wrecks. The masts and spars are still standing, and the crew are there, but the master is gone, and the tide on which the ship floated has receded, leaving her high and dry, her cordage rotting, and her hulk beginning to crumble to dust and nothingness. Names of places need not be given;

they will be only too readily recognised by those who know the history of African Missions. To ensure permanent success and stability for the future Church, the European element must be continued for generations. The foreign missionary ought to become more the superintendent or bishop, while the practical daily work should be undertaken almost entirely by native pastors and evangelists. Till this is done, much energy will be wasted in attending to details which could be done with a good measure of efficiency by subordinates and assistants.

About this time I found myself in the excitement of new experiences. Early in January a native man came to report that there had been a fatal shooting accident six miles from Lovedale, and that a young man named Murray had been conveyed to prison by the native headman. Dr. Stewart and I proceeded to the spot, and found that five native girls had gone to a farm-house, where they had been accustomed to get oranges and lemons from an old Irishman who took charge in the absence of the owner. On this occasion they were met at the door by the owner's son, who had just arrived. On hearing their request he ordered them away, but they continued to plead for permission to take a few. Murray then picked up a gun, and said, "Get away, or I shall shoot you." One of the girls replied, "We would rather go than that, but do please give us a few." There is not much more to tell. There was a flash of light, a sharp report, and three lives were quenched in darkness. They had been standing in line before him, and the buckshot with which the gun was charged did its work only too well.

I shall never forget the scene in the house of death. The three bodies lay on the ground, covered with blankets. The father of two of the girls, a Christian man, Hai-hai by name, sat in a corner. When we entered he rose to greet Dr. Stewart, whom he knew, and briefly told us his sad story. We could do nothing to help him, and little to console.

Murray was tried and acquitted of all blame. The verdict gave satisfaction to no one; but Hai-hai put it thus: "My children are taken from me, and I cannot bring them back. I will go away to forget I had any." Not so Peit, the father of the third girl; he cherished a grudge, and sought for revenge. Whether he obtained it I do not know; but one day during the war of 1877, young Murray was found dead, a few miles from his father's house, where he had ridden out to drive home some cattle. By whose hand he fell no one can tell, but I have never been able to rid my mind of the idea that there was a connection between the first tragic scene I had witnessed in Africa, and the mangled body found in the African jungle. Such deeply-shaded pictures have made Africa a land of woe and lamentation since first the white man trod its solitary wastes. Wrong, oppression, and commerce in human flesh has left a record which Europe in tears could not wipe off the page of history.

It was arranged in January that Dr. Stewart and I should proceed together to the Transkei, which was to be the sphere of my future labours, and, after the necessary preparation, we started on our journey. We lodged for the first night at a place bearing a name of evil omen—Hangman's Bush. The hotel, however, proved to be comfortable and its fare excellent. The following day, we passed through the valley of the Kei, one of the deepest river gorges in the Colony. The land on both sides of the valley consists of open rolling plains and grassy meadows, and through this runs the river, more than 2000 feet below the level of the surrounding country. One comes quite unexpectedly to the edge of the valley, and the descent is both rough and precipitous. The road winds about the hill sides in a curious zig-zag, running here and there into the narrow chasms which have been hollowed out of the mountain side by the action of torrents. The slopes are thickly wooded, and many tropical plants are found in odd corners. Troops of monkeys are often seen among the trees and rocks, and numerous antelopes hide away in the depths of the forest. At the date of my visit, trees and shrubs were in full bloom; and the purple of the walnut, the scarlet of the Kaffir boom, the yellow of the different varieties of acacia, and the crimson flower of the common aloe made a most pleasing picture. The whole scene had a grandeur and luxuriance about it, such as I had not hitherto seen in the country. The road was broken and uneven, and I had to walk at two or three bad bits, but this only added to my opportunity of observing the beauty of the scene, and the richness of colouring which filled in the picture of brilliant flower and dark forest with grey weather-worn rocks and scaurs.

At the spot where we crossed the river is not more than 150 yards wide, but, when in flood, it spreads over the gravelly bed to a width of a quarter of a mile. A magnificent iron bridge now spans the river. Our "spider" was ferried over by a German son of Charon at a charge of twelve shillings, and the two passengers for half-a-crown. Of a Kaffir predecessor of his I heard a good story. He ferried his own countrymen at sixpence each, Englishmen at a shilling, and Germans at eighteenpence. One of the latter nationality is said, after the first introduction of the florin pieces, to have imported a large number, and distributed them among the unsuspecting Kaffirs as half-crowns. To this day, a florin is known by no other name than a "German" among them. Our friend, the ferryman, may have been like the Scotchman who agreed to hang a man for the authorities at Carlisle, after they had tried in vain to get a townsman to do it, on the ground that it would be "doing something to pay back for Flodden."

From the Kei, we drove to Cunningham, a distance of fourteen miles. This was the earliest of our Transkei Stations, founded by the Rev. Richard Ross. The mission-house is a good large stone building. The native church looked a rather dilapidated wattle and daub structure, sadly in need of repair or renewal. Both stand near the junction of two small streams in a fertile but uninteresting valley. Mr. Ross has, however, made the most of the site, and has surrounded his house with an extensive grove of oaks, blue gums, and about fifty orange trees. The latter are both ornamental and useful. They can, besides, be made a source of revenue in favourable circumstances.

After resting and receiving every kindness at the mission-house, we proceeded to Blythswood where we met Mrs. Stewart, who had, with her children, preceded us in a waggon. Besides the waggon she had for accommodation a small sod hut about ten feet square, and in this "house that Jack built," she entertained us during our stay in the district.

The situation of Blythswood though central is, in some respects, unsatisfactory. The country round is treeless and uninteresting, the streams of water are weak and can never be used for irrigation in connection with agricultural operations and tree planting. Fuel is difficult to obtain. These considerations apart, the spot is in every respect suitable for its intended purpose, and may in after years, if clothed with timber, be greatly beautified and improved. The walls at this time were but a few feet above the foundation, and gave no idea of the handsome appearance of the completed edifice.

The tradesmen employed were four stone masons

from Aberdeen, imported by the Mission authorities specially for the work. Before leaving their native city, they, like prudent Scotchmen, had provided themselves with a blunderbuss a-piece to wage war on lions and tigers. One of them told me pathetically that it "was a' deid money for there's nothing to shoot." Their hardships were dilated upon at length, they had been sent up with a tent, and had to " sit down in a park where they could get no lodgings and no body to bake bread." Cattle got among their tent ropes, and they erected "scratching posts" to keep them away from their camp. The first stormy night the tent "geid clean owre our heids, and left us in our beds in the rain," and "they natives are just a wheen pock puddins who try to get the lend o' ye in a' thing." Isolation and solitude will in time affect the best ordered minds, and our Aberdonian friends, before finishing their work at Blythswood, had a good many difficulties to contend with, some of which they settled with their fists in a manner that would have shocked the douce elder who selected them as sober and pious young men. The work was, however, completed, and the building formally opened about a year and a-half after my first visit to the district. Of this and the history of Blythswood, I shall have something to say in another place. I shall also defer, in the meantime, a detailed notice of the native people with whom I met, and among whom I was to live and work.

It was our intention to return to the Colony on a

Monday, but on that day, and for three days previously, it rained as if Jupiter Pluvius had taken up his permanent abode directly overhead. Scotch "mist," or even Scotch "showry weather," one can regard with complacency, and a good African tornado is endurable, but when it comes to a four days' steady downpour, without a breath of wind or change of appearance, or colour from a deep leaden hue over the limited space visible, one's philosophy is apt to be at fault, and impatience gives place to downright ill-natured grumbling. It has been said that one feels need of that solace under trials, which a Scotch wife suggested when the Bishop called and found her and her "guid man" riddling corn in the barn. John in his haste to greet the Bishop trampled on the rim of the riddle, which rebounded and struck him violently on the shin. He rubbed the limb, grinned and danced about, but could not utter a word. The wife came to the rescue and advised the Bishop to "gang his ways into the house till John has an opportunity of relieving his feelings wi' an aith or twa, and he will be wi' ye in a minute."

It was not till Wednesday morning we could leave our quarters, and even then every streamlet was a torrent, and every river looked like a prolonged lake. With perseverance and patience we reached King William's Town at noon on Friday, and on the following morning I took my seat in a "Cobb's" for Graham's Town, where I was to supply ordinances in the Presbyterian Church for a month or two. When about half-way, and going at a good pace, one of the wheels met with an obstruction and away we went, coach, passengers, mail-bags and baggage in one confused heap down a steep muddy bank. No one was seriously hurt. A Captain Bailie sat next to me, and in falling I alighted right on his back. The humour of the situation was too much for him, and he, as he struggled to regain his feet, exclaimed, "Man, could you not find a bit of country to fall upon except my back!" After an hour's hard work the vehicle was righted, and we were bowling along as merrily as if nothing had happened. My adventures for the day were not over. The bridge across the Fish river had been swept away by a flood the previous year, and the one meant to replace it, a large structure of five arches, was not completed. Passengers and mails were at the river transferred to another coach, and the means of crossing was as follows:—A stout wire rope was stretched from bank to bank, and on this there was a travelling cradle in which two persons at a time could cross. When I reached the opposite bank I stepped out of the cradle on to the slippery clay, and losing my footing landed in the water. There was no danger, but in this plight I sat for over three hours in a broiling sun till we reached our destination. The following morning I awoke with shivering and fever. This was my only severe attack of the kind all the years I spent in Africa.

My Graham's Town visit I enjoyed immensely. I was introduced to the best families in both town and country round about, and the days passed pleasantly and all too swiftly. In the same hotel with me lived R. M. Ballantyne, who was collecting material for his " Settler and Savage," and his companionship I found as charming as his books are delightful. At Graham's Town he was very favourably situated for the purpose he had in view. At that time a goodly number of the settlers of 1820 still lived, and delighted in recounting stories of the early days, when Albany was a wilderness, and lions could be found in what is now the paved streets of Graham's Town. Through this fortunate meeting, I came to know more of early settler life than I could ever have learned from Parliamentary Blue Books and official dispatches; but though the subject is a tempting one, I must not enter upon it.

I returned to Lovedale in March, much the better of the change, and with widened knowledge and sympathy regarding that moot point, the relation of colonist to native. I could now understand the feeling of bitterness many otherwise estimable people have towards the natives, and how the action of a handful of stock thieves have entailed upon their countrymen many bloody reprisals, and finally the loss of name and country. Frontier history is a much more complicated affair than the respective advocates of natives and colonists would have us believe. The former can see in it nothing but land hunger and spoliation; the latter nothing but Kaffir treachery and inveterate lying. A calm and impartial discussion of the question is at present impossible, and any one attempting it would be abused by both parties. When the history comes to be fully written, it will be found that blame attaches equally to both, or rather the blame shall be found to rest primarily with the respective civilised Governments, Dutch and English, who professed to rule and protect the frontier, and at the same time, neither ruled the farmers nor kept the natives in check. Irresponsible action, injustice, and cheating were followed by stock thefts; these again, by commandos, reprisals and bloodshed, while dispatches were written in Cape Town which commanded the same respect that a royal mandate did in the territories of the Lord of the Isles six centuries ago. Such continued to be the case down to the days of Sir G. Grey, as Governor at the Cape. Since then a strong and resolute hand has, on the whole, held rule on the frontier.

During the year 1876, the work at Lovedale proceeded quietly. There was expansion in various directions, but nothing worthy of special remark. In August Dr. Stewart was instructed to proceed to Livingstonia. The new Institution Buildings, erected at great cost, were commenced, and the troubles at Blythswood, in view of events at Lovedale, appeared but as a breeze before the full blast of the hurricane. We had imported a second batch of masons from Aberdeen, but from the first day difficulties arose or were created. No sooner was one dispute settled than another cropped up, nor was there any disposition to attempt smooth and harmonious working. A man sent out as foreman stone-mason, turned out to have been originally a shoemaker! Another worthy could neither fix a mason's guiding line on the wall, nor lay his stones correctly, when some one else did it for him. If a man, dressing a stone, was shown by compass and square, that it was neither the shape nor size shown on the plan from which he was working, he, as likely as not, dropped his tools and said, "Ye better try it yersel'." No one who has not had experience of it, can have any conception of the difficulty of getting good work done under such circumstances. If I were to transfer to these pages a detailed record of our difficulties, comical doings, and law suits, as I wrote them down at the time, it would read like a romance, and would simply not be believed by the majority of readers. Fortunately one or two of us knew something about building, and insisted on fair work being done; but from the very quarrying of the stones to the building of the simplest plain wall, constant vigilance had to be exercised, and one could be sure of nothing that was to be out of sight.

For six months I was constantly on the road between Lovedale and Blythswood, a distance of about 120 miles, looking after building operations and settling disputes and difficulties. One day the tradesmen quarrelled among themselves; the next it was a dispute with native labourers; or again, it was a question of pulling down what had been badly built. The work was ultimately finished, but few of those who support Missions have any adequate idea of the difficulty of getting any large undertaking carried to a successful issue, in distant and inaccessible regions.

IV.

THE TRANSKEI—BLYTHSWOOD.

BLYTHSWOOD is situated about one hundred and twenty miles north-east of Lovedale, in that section of the Transkei territory known as Fingoland. Its origin and history form an interesting chapter in the record of modern Missions. To trace this clearly, a brief sketch of the history of the Fingoes must be given. They are the broken remnants of tribes scattered by war during the reigns of Tshaka and Dingan in Zululand, and who, in their flight southward, found an asylum among the Gcalekas and Tembus, who reduced them to the position of domestic slaves.

During the troublesome times between 1830 and 1857, the Fingoes in large numbers entered the Colony, and were allotted locations in the districts of Victoria, Beaufort, and Peddie, where they prospered and became industrious, both in tillage and stock rearing. Missions were planted among them, and many embraced Christianity and adopted civilised habits of life. Their liberty brought them one curse, namely, an unlimited supply of Cape brandy, and this acted like a running sore, preventing the accumulation of wealth, and sending many to untimely graves. They, however, increased rapidly in numbers, and it was found, about twenty-five years ago, that the locations held by them were much too small for the population to live comfortably and honestly on the products of the soil. Large tracts of unoccupied land were held by the Colonial Government in the Transkei, and it was decided to offer such as cared to emigrate a section of this territory. Candidates for land were not wanting, and numbers were located in the Transkei under the care of a "Fingoe Resident" or Government representative.

From the day on which they took possession of the new country, the Fingoes of the Transkei entered on a career of material progress and moral development unparalleled in the history of any other African tribe. They were now free from many of the Colonial facilities for self-indulgence and vice. The sale of strong drink among them was strictly prohibited, and the Act regarding it was administered with a hand of iron. Brandy became an unknown article. Under the direction of the Resident they began to make material improvements. The territory was practically inaccessible to wheeled vehicles owing to the difficulties of crossing the valley of the Kei. The Fingoes contributed £1000, and made a good passable if primitive road. They cut long water races, and brought the best of their arable land under irrigation, village schools were erected by the people, and something was contributed by many head men towards a teacher's salary. The cultivation of wheat, oats, potatoes, and other cereals for market made satisfactory progress, and the people were prosperous and contented.

Captain Blyth, who succeeded Captain Cobb, having made such a successful beginning, thought it a pity if the whole national energy should be represented by a rough mountain road and a few village schools, entered into a correspondence with Dr. Stewart of Lovedale about a project for a school on a larger scale than anything hitherto attempted eastward of the Kei. Several claim, or claims have been made on their behalf, to have originated the idea of Blythswood in its present form. It is not my province to decide between them. I was not in the country at the time, and personally know nothing about it. That Captain Blyth, the Rev. Richard Ross, and Dr. Stewart had a hand in it is clear, but the part taken by each is far from apparent. This much is certain, that without Captain Blyth there could have been no Blythswood, and that Dr. Stewart gave the project form and shape, and also, both in Africa and in Scotland, was the principal agent in carrying the idea to a successful issue.

Be the history what it may, the fact on which I wish to concentrate attention is, that at a public meeting of the whole Fingoe people, it was resolved that every man liable to be taxed, should contribute five shillings towards the proposed building. This sum they again repeated twice told, so that in all, each man, Christian and heathen, paid a sum of fifteen shillings for the erection of a public Missionary Institution, making a total of over £4000 sterling. This was done by a people to whom the idea was absolutely new, and of whom many disapproved of education, and were violently opposed to Christianity. To the £4000 contributed by the Fingoes, the Free Church of Scotland added an almost equal amount, and erected a building which is a fitting monument of a noble effort made in such exceptional circumstances.

The magnitude of the effort made, and the departure from traditional usage it implied, will be better understood if we bear in mind the state of native feeling at the time in regard to Christianity, education and progress in the arts and habits of civilised life. Among the Fingoes in the Colony there was a small party who had received less or more education, and who were active and persistent advocates of progress. In their ranks were many who openly scoffed at the ancient faith and practice as represented by witchcraft and the fear of departed spirits. There was also a Christian community, very small it is true, but having enthusiasm and untiring energy. Among them were several very able and capable men who wielded wide influence, irrespective of differences of creed and custom. On the other hand, there was a vast mass of inert heathenism. This was nominally under the control of the magicians as in former days, and they succeeded, now and again, to rouse the national apathy into a kind of galvanised life and activity. But all such efforts were spasmodic, and plainly told that the ancient cult had become *effeté*, and could never again, under existing circumstances, become a national religion, nor a time-honoured philosophy. Contact with Europeans had fatally undermined the traditional faith, and had substituted nothing in its place, and efforts made to revive and re-establish customary usage only helped to bring ridicule upon persons, who, a few years before, were regarded as a sacred order.

All this was closely watched by the conservative and reactionary party. They saw their wives converted to Christianity, and their daughters attending school irrespective of their wishes, and then refusing to be sold for cattle as wives to men they cared nothing for, and perhaps never even saw. They saw young men scoffing openly at ghosts and goblins having power over life, death, or fortune. Pools sacred to malignant water spirits were converted into swimming ponds by school boys with the schoolmasters at their head. European dress was to be seen in every village, and women in calico gowns dared even to approach the "great place" of headmen. Chemists' apprentices sneered at witch-doctors who "extracted" disease, or "smelt out" the wizard causing it, and undertook the duty themselves "wi' drap and pill." This being the state of matters in the Colony, when the Transkei was proclaimed open to all wishing to take advantage of it, the heathen and conservative section of the headmen were the first to come forward. They wished to leave the Colony, and retire to a region where they could gather round them those only who were in sympathy with themselves.

After the emigration, events proved too strong for them. The Brandy Prohibition Act made them sober, and on this followed material prosperity and substantial wealth. To men so circumstanced the advantages of education could not but be apparent. The contrast between themselves and other tribes was too sharp and well defined to be missed. Headmen who fled from Mission stations to avoid their influence, now began to feel that material prosperity did not satisfy the aspirations of their people, and that their only chance of retaining their authority and commanding the respect of the community, was in putting themselves in line with the new movement, and becoming advocates of that which in their hearts they at the same time dreaded and despised. These complex influences which moved the people produced results which have proved highly satisfactory, and to-day the Fingoes of the Transkei are half a century ahead of their countrymen in wealth, intelligence, material progress, agricultural skill, sobriety, and civilised habits of life, both in food, clothing, and dwellings.

It was decided by those in charge of the undertaking to hold the ceremonial opening of Blythswood on the 25th of July. To give something of a national character to the event, a good number—over twenty, I think—of oxen, and about a dozen sheep and goats were slaughtered, and a committee appointed to superintend the arrangements, and see that provision was made for not fewer than 3000 guests.

The opening day happened to be exceptionally stormy. From early morning there was a regular tornado of wind and dust. Those in charge of the cooking, which was done outside, could not keep their fires burning, and the young men and boys in attendance, instead of running actively about, cowered for shelter behind every object they could find. I feared the attendance would be small and the meeting a failure, but, by 11 A.M., when the short preliminary service began, there were over two thousand people present. At the close of the service, Mr. James Ayliff, the Resident who had succeeded Captain Blyth, took the chair and made a long statement of the history of the Institution. I took notes at the time, but, in the confusion of the war which followed, they were lost. I do not remember very much of what he said, but I do recollect his appealing to their past history as slaves to the Gcalekas, after they had been dispersed by Tshaka, and pointing to the large number of magistrates, missionaries, and merchants on the platform as an evidence of the interest taken in their future welfare by the European community. The following brief account taken from the *Cape Mercury* is, so far as I know, the only extant record of the day's proceedings. The writer says:—

"This Institution was publicly opened on Wednesday, the 25th inst. There were about 4000 natives, and a considerable number of Europeans present. The opening sermon was preached by the Rev. P. Mazimba, of Lovedale, after which J. Ayliff, Esq., took the chair. In introducing the business of the day, Mr. Ayliff made reference to what the Fingoe people had already done since they first occupied their present land. He explained the benefit they had derived from the roads they made, and the increased wealth brought to their country by means of these roads; how the hut tax, at which so many grumbled, assured them of the protection of the British Government, and asked them every time they saw the national ensign, which then waved over the building, to think of what they were before the Government took them, and of what they are now. The chairman then proceeded to explain how and why such institutions as the one they were met to open were erected, and how that work would spread and go on for ever, following those who flew away from it go where they would, and not only so, but roads and bridges would follow them to their new homes, and they would have to help to make them. Mr. Ayliff concluded his speech by paying a high compliment to the character of the men who have been engaged at the building.

"The financial statement was then read by Rev. J. Macdonald, of Blythswood. From the statement it appears that the Fingoes have in all paid nearly £3000 towards the erection of the Institution, and that £1500 was collected in Scotland for the same purpose by Dr. Stewart, and a sum of £700 sent by the Foreign Missions Committee subsequently to Mr. Macdonald. The entire cost of the building has been over £7000, and the present debt about £1600.

"The building, which is of rough ashlar, is 200 feet long by 40 feet wide. It consists of two stories, the lower one containing a hall 60 feet by 40, the missionary's dwelling-house, and several class-rooms and dormitories. The upper story consists entirely of dormitories, those above the dwelling-house being meant for Europeans, and those above the hall and class-rooms for natives. Accommodation can be given, when the building is completed, to about 120 native and 30 European boarders.

"At the meeting about £300 was contributed in money or in kind, and the people expressed their willingness to bear their share of the debt by giving another subscription.

"The Institution reflects the greatest credit on the Fingoe people, and also on those who were its promoters. It plainly shows what can be done by a united effort, and points the way to what may be accomplished among other tribes.

"Capt. Blyth, whose name is so intimately connected with the Institution, in expressing his regret at not being able to be present, said that nothing has ever given him greater pleasure or pride than being connected with its erection.

"We hope the Institution will prove in every way worthy of its noble object—viz., giving a sound education and an industrial training to the native youths of the country. And we trust that if European youths mingle with them in educational work, it may be the means of raising a better class feeling, and removing the mutual distrust that at present exists. That the natives, trained and enlightened, will no longer think of war, but come to see that their strength lies in peace and the continued friendship of the white race."

After the financial statement was read, the native people were invited to take part in the proceedings. One orator after another rose, and began by praising

Queen Victoria's rule, and pointing to a magnificent ensign, the gift of Miss B. Birrell of Carlisle, floating from the flagstaff on the building, professed undying loyalty to the Queen's person and Government, and finished by depositing a contribution on the table, or promising to send sheep, goat, or ox for the benefit of the Institution.

At the close of the public meeting, the head men and their immediate retainers were invited into the hall of the Institution where an ample supply of beef, Indian corn, bread and coffee was provided for them. The multitude were served outside with beef and Indian corn. I was in attendance upon the great men, and could not see what was going on outside, but in an incredibly short space of time, the flesh of our twenty oxen disappeared under the united exertions of some three thousand pairs of human jaws, and when all was finished many asked for more. What they could not eat pockets would conveniently accommodate. Inside the hall the Babel was deafening. Every one could not be waited upon at once, and those who were not served instantly, imagined that the supply would not be sufficient for all, or that they were neglected, and shouted frantically to the waiters for beef, coffee or bread. At last the sounds diminished, and as I stood looking down the long rows of tables, I felt amazed at the rapidity with which junks of beef were made to disappear. The diminished requests for further supplies, told that good solid food was having its usual effect even when Fingoe stomachs were in question. But if any European knowing nothing of savage or semi-savage life, had been in that hall, and had seen the mountains of beef that disappeared, he would have concluded that before morning there would be ample work for the doctors, with a trifle left over for the coroner. The paramount chief of the Tembus, Gangilizwe, was present as a guest. As the greatest and most distinguished man in the room, he must have some taste or fancy peculiar to himself. When coffee was served, he sent a message by the waiter to say that Gangilizwe did not drink coffee, but a bowl of tea would be very welcome. Mr. Ayliff and I were standing together at the coffee caldrons at the moment. I ordered a servant to infuse some tea; Mr. Ayliff thought this quite unnecessary, and filling a large bowl with steaming coffee, he added a good handful of tea and dispatched this decoction to our august guest. He drank the poison, smacked his lips with satisfaction, and desired his special thanks to be conveyed to the lady in charge who had sent him such an excellent dish of tea.

After dinner the usual loyal and complimentary speeches were made. The oratory was both fervent and eloquent. Mutual congratulations and flattery passed and repassed like current coin. Every one seemed pleased with himself and with his relations to other men. No regard was paid to ominous sounds which had been heard, and the absence of Kreli after receiving a special invitation, was hardly noticed. The cloud on the horizon "not bigger than a man's hand," was, however, destined to develop in a few months into a violent tempest. A tempest which lasted for full five years, and changed much of the frontier from its former conditions into new and different relations.

V.

PEACE—DIPLOMACY—WAR.

FOR a few brief weeks after the opening ceremonies, the Institution presented the ordinary appearance of a well-equipped school, but by the beginning of October, Blythswood had become a harbour of refuge, and centre of military operations. The causes which led to hostilities it would be tedious to trace. Oldstanding jealousies between Gcalekas and Fingoes could have no other termination, and though the immediate cause of the outbreak was contemptible enough, it had long been felt that war was inevitable.

On the 3rd of August, a social party for feasting and beer-drinking was given by a Fingoe of good standing, living near the border, at which a number of Gcalekas were present. The feast was on a liberal scale, and the bowl passed and repassed with a frequency which boded evil. It is said brandy was added to the beer to give it flavour and potency, and that early in the afternoon, most of the guests were in a state of semi-intoxication. Towards sunset the host, according to custom, took a well-filled flagon, and after drinking from it, passed it to one of the principal guests for a parting drink, and a sign that it was now time to disperse and return to their homes. The meeting was thus formally dissolved, but many were too far advanced in intoxication to understand very clearly what was being done. Some Gcaleka youths demanded more beer, which was refused as a violation of custom, and being contrary to all rules of hospitality. It was also thought by the master of the house, who was sober, to be undesirable on other grounds. The refusal was resented, and a scuffle followed, in which a three-legged iron pot was broken. This roused the resentment of the Fingoe youths present, and sticks and stones were used on both sides with vigour and effect. In the melee two of the guests were severely wounded, and one of them died during the night. This the Gcaleka sub-chief, Xoxo, regarded as an insult which could only be wiped out in blood. He accordingly organised a raid into Fingoland, in which several men were shot, and a large number of cattle driven off by the assailants.

This was too serious to be lightly regarded, and Mr. Ayliff, the Fingoe Resident, proceeded without delay to investigate the matter on the spot, and demand restitution of the cattle. On the border all was excitement. Every man was armed, and Fingoes and Gcalekas seemed equally determined to fight. After much anxious negotiation he persuaded the Fingoes to retire from the border. The Gcalekas also promised to return to their homes till such time as an inquiry could be held, and that meantime they would collect the cattle which had been stolen, with a view to their restoration. Neither promise was kept. The appearance of a peaceful settlement was but the lull before the storm. Continued peace was impossible, for no one wanted peace.

The Residents in the respective districts meantime arranged for a joint-court of inquiry to be held at Butterworth. On the day appointed they met, and opened the inquiry with no small ceremony and show of authority. Evidence was heard in that calm, deliberate, and judicial manner peculiar to the higher law Courts. Day after day passed, and not much progress was made—the braves on either side fretting like hounds in leash. The Court covered reams of foolscap with evidence as to who broke the pot, and whether a Fingoe or Gcaleka cast the first stone. Then it was essential to know whether the Fingoes, in the original scuffle, crossed the boundary into Gcalekaland or not, and whether this man and that were, at the time, so drunk that their evidence could not be accepted. The quantity of beer made, and the exact number of bottles of brandy added, was also a point which needed elucidation.

On the last day on which this extraordinary Court sat a comical scene was enacted. Towards afternoon the loungers seemed roused to an unwonted state of excitement and activity. Men entered and left the Court-room at short intervals with excited looks and almost defiant manner, and the witnesses could hardly be got to give attention to the questions put; their ears seemed turned in other directions. Sinister rumours filled the air, and every one was on the alert for news and expecting something important to happen.

And something did happen. About 2.30 P.M. news came, and in the unwelcome and alarming form of a sharp and sustained fire of musketry at no great distance. Every one was thunderstruck. The audience rushed to the doors and ran to their weapons. The witness in the box began to harangue the Court. The president looked serious and adjourned the inquiry, while most of those present made their way to the scene of action.

The fighting was not attended with such serious consequences as might be inferred from the noise. When men, armed with smooth bore guns, are posted on two hill sides a thousand yards apart, the slaughter cannot be very great. But though no damage was done the fact was too significant to be neglected.

Once more attempts were made to effect a reconciliation. The Fingoes were disposed to listen to reason, but the Gcalekas seemed bent on war. Days were spent in palavers. Kreli did not attend these, but now and again sent a message to say *he* did not wish for war. Some thought that in this he was sincere, and that it held out a prospect of peace. The event proved that the old chief had determined upon war long before this date, and only sought to gain time to complete his arrangements and cement the compact with those other tribes who had promised him their support.

Before negotiations were finally broken off the Governor of the Colony arranged to pay a visit to the district, and if possible, by personal influence, restore order and confidence. It was intimated that such visit was intended, and this caused a cessation in the raiding and skirmishing going on between the residents on the respective borders. But the longer negotiations were protracted the more complicated did the situation become. Early in September Sir Bartle Frere arrived in the Transkei and proceeded slowly to Butterworth. His leisurely movements allowed the news of his arrival to spread, and being devoid of escort confidence was in some measure restored. It was then hoped that the whole affair would resolve itself into a mere question of police supervision and more effectual administration on the borders. When the party reached Butterworth a messenger was dispatched to inform Kreli that the Governor had arrived, and wished to hold a conference with him at a place named. The wily Kaffir made excuses. He was not satisfied with the place of meeting chosen, and he wished to delay and return an answer the following day. In this way several days were spent, messengers passing and repassing at short intervals. As a last resort Sir Bartle Frere sent the Hon. Charles Brownlee to meet with Kreli, and if possible arrange satisfactory terms of peace. After much preliminary talking and palaver, Kreli, who was attended by a division of his army, asked, "Can your Governor show such a tail as that?" The hint was too plain to be misunderstood, and though the chief professed an earnest desire for peace, Brownlee knew that the chances of permanent peace were at an end.

After the failure of the negotiations with Kreli and his refusal to meet the Governor, the party proceeded to Blythswood partly for the purpose of visiting the Institution, and also with the view of holding a mass meeting of Fingoes. During his stay, the Governor and his staff were our guests at the Mission-house. He expressed his cordial approval of the work of the Institution and the objects aimed at. While at Blythswood, he visited a cave of peculiar interest in the vicinity. This had once been the home of a tribe of wandering bushmen, and on its rocky sides, they have left a series of rude drawings which have defied the ravages of time to efface them. The colours, when grime and dirt were washed away, proved to be as fresh as when left by the hand of the savage artist. The drawings are of men—both in the attitude of warriors, dancers, and as stalkers of game —oxen, various species of antelope, elephants, hippopotami, and ostriches, and they are painted in white, terra cotta, brown of various shades, and a pigment verging upon black. Whence they obtained their colours, or with what ingredients they mixed them, no one knows. The art, rude as it was, has been lost, and many eminent men have puzzled over the secret in vain. I had the drawings referred to copied, and sent them to Sir Bartle Frere, who was greatly interested in the habits and customs of savage and semi-savage peoples.

On the appointed day, a mass meeting of Fingoes was held. There was a very large attendance, but several well-known headmen of tried and proved loyalty were absent. These lived near the Gcaleka border, and though their non-appearance was significant, it was not much noticed. Sir Bartle Frere, in a long address, explained the position so far as it had developed itself. He assured the Fingoes of support in the last resort, and counselled them to retire to their homes. They were not to go near the border, and if found provoking Gcalekas to acts of violence, they were to be severely punished. A rigid inquiry would be made into recent disturbances, and whoever should be found guilty must bear the blame and suffer the penalty inflicted. Those who had suffered wrong would receive all redress and compensation that could in the circumstances be given. As is usual on important occasions, there was a good deal of talk, and such flattering speeches, as only Kaffirs can make, were made in reply to the Governor's address. A new name was invented for him, and a local bard sang his praises in a few stanzas of smooth flowing verse. After this peace programme was laid down and approved with acclamation, the whole party moved slowly towards the Colony. But though Sir Bartle Frere urged the Fingoes to preserve the peace, and spoke as if war were almost an impossibility, his

Indian experience had taught him the necessity of taking precautionary measures.

At the moment when the Governor was urging the Fingoes to return to their ploughing and wheat sowing, and to study how to improve the breed of their horses and cattle, John Masimisa, whose absence had been noticed, was at the head of his followers fighting a rather stubborn battle to repel an incursion of Gcalekas into his location. The news of this engagement reached the Colony before the Governor, and caused no small consternation there.

The din of preparation now began. Troops were moved towards the frontier; volunteers were called out, and a definite programme laid down for the conduct of the coming war. There was still no open rupture retween the Gcalekas and the Colony, and hopes of peace were entertained by some. Negotiations were once more opened, till all hope of a friendly adjustment was cut short by the action of an over-zealous police-officer. This man had an inordinate conceit of the prowess of the Frontier Mounted Police. With fifty men he would march through Kaffir land and defeat the biggest army Kreli could put in the field. Shells and rockets would scatter them like sheep worried by wolves, and as for their hiding-places in the forest, why, it would be the simplest thing imaginable to shell them out of their strongholds. On the present occasion he was ordered to patrol the border for a distance of twenty miles or thereby. He had with him a troop of twenty-five men, and a mountain gun under the charge of a non-commissioned officer. At a spot called Gwadana he found that there had been a brisk skirmish between Fingoes and Gcalekas that same morning, and without more ado, he proceeded to chastise the latter, who had some hours before retired to their own country. He advanced along a grassy ridge. The Gcalekas accepted the challenge, and marched boldly to meet him. The shells and rockets instead of striking terror into the hearts of the savage warriors, were received with the derisive cheer, *Wabotshwa*—It is nothing. They quickened their step, firing as they ran. Seven policemen fell fighting; the others, in confusion, ran to their horses, and were got into something like order by a subaltern, who conducted them to Idutywa, a broken and spiritless party.

The report of the doings at Gwadana spread consternation far and wide. Europeans who had been urged to remain at their stations, and not remove any of their goods, felt as if they had been betrayed. Three days before they could have left with their all; now they found themselves at the mercy of the enemy, and glad to escape with bare life. Days must elapse before troops could arrive from King William's Town, and after the Gwadana the police were too much demoralised to do much outside their barrack yards. Luckily Colonel Eustace, who had seen much guerrilla warfare in Turkey, was at Ibeka, and though acting in a civil capacity, did much to restore confidence, and to direct those in charge of military affairs. It was decided to direct all refugees to repair to Blythswood, while I was instructed to do all in my power to put the place into a state of defence. Assistance was promised at the earliest possible date, and meantime my own tradesmen, apprentices, and such refugees, as might be able and willing to work, were to be employed. The Resident, Mr. James Ayliff, conveyed these instructions to Blythswood. His visit was brief, and after he had gone, I called the boys together, and told them they were to pack up and make ready for an early start to their homes on the morrow. The tradesmen I directed to begin making wooden barricades for the doors and windows. The arrangements were quietly made, and not a man uttered a grumble or sought to shirk the duties and dangers of the situation by a timely flight to the Colony. In forty-eight hours we had made barricades for every door and window of the lowest story of the building, and were in a position to offer a stout resistance should we be attacked.

It was not long after we had received our instructions when the first refugees arrived. Such accommodation as could be given was very limited. In no case could more than one room be given to a single family, and to some even that meagre comfort could not be assigned. Many had to sleep in the hall and in outhouses, and cook as best they could in the open air. The characteristics of individuals were shown in a most remarkable manner during the first day or two. Some arrived in waggons, having saved most of their household goods, and clamoured loudly and insolently for storage room for the stuff; such demands had to be sternly refused. Others again, realising the rights of those who had not yet arrived, proceeded to pile up their goods outside, and even offered tents and waggons to supplement our scanty accommodation for those who reached us utterly destitute. The later arrivals were Gcalekaland traders, who were not allowed to bring away any article of value, and who, for the most part, arrived on foot. Most of them were well-to-do people, and very well able to pay for whatever they required, but it was none the less difficult to provide for them on this account. Goods were at famine prices, and certain necessaries could not be had at any price. A good many single men came on horseback, and gave most effectual assistance in organising a local Volunteer corps. Their stay was, however, brief, being drafted off to the border to engage in the more serious business of actual war.

A number of families from Idutywa, a district to the east of Fingoland, and where disaffection had spread, were expected at Blythswood. When, after forty-eight hours, they had not arrived, we got anxious—almost alarmed for their safety—I sent parties of men, with transport oxen, to meet them; but it was not till the afternoon of the third day that their advanced guard arrived, under the guise of a drunken doctor of medicine—a poor waif sent out by his friends, and who led a miserable life on the frontier. He reported their whereabouts, somewhat incoherently, and early in the night their waggons began to arrive, and we were very glad to see them safely in camp.

After a few days were spent in reducing chaos to cosmos, most of the men—the sick, lame, and lazy excepted—went to the border as volunteers. When I took a census of my increased family, I found there were 173 women and children, several old men, and a few active hands retained for necessary duty. There were also fifteen men of the Cape police stationed at Blythswood, to be at hand in case of emergencies.

The allocation of space among so many, and the adjustment of rival claims was, by no means, a simple matter, and in spite of all I could do, there were heartburnings and grumblings. Among the refugees from Idutywa was a Mrs. Prichard, who subsequently published a book giving her experiences of this time. Of her arrival at Blythswood, and what met her there, she says:—

"I now began to feel excessively nervous about our reception at Blythswood, and I sincerely wished it could still have been my lot to have remained in my own house and be in a position to offer, instead of ask, for shelter and hospitality.

"Mrs. Eustace did her best to infuse brightness and courage in every direction. Some, however, refused to be comforted, and soon the two sets divided, the melancholy mortals being left to weep at will on one side of the room, while those who joined Mrs. Eustace's 'band of hope' preferred the sunny side, and clustered about, laughing over our various adventures, and relating the experiences which had befallen us all during the two previous days.

"Mr. Macdonald, the Principal, now entered the room—the hall of the Institution had been converted into a kind of general reception room—and was greeted with smiles on his right hand, and by tears and sighs on his left. He seemed to prefer sunshine to cloud, for, on apportioning to each lady her apartment and position in the house, we found, to our amusement, that smiles had the best of it, and dear Mrs. Eustace at once took possession of the very large room, at that moment used as a drawing-room, while a most charming apartment, at the end of the corridor, was allotted to me. I rather pitied Mr. Macdonald, for his position was somewhat trying; rival claims appeared on every hand, and he must have known that, however he decided, he must annoy some. He did not, however, allow himself to be influenced or disturbed in any way, and having quietly but firmly made his own arrangements, went upstairs to divide the vacant space there among the families, who crowded every yard of available space."

Mrs. Prichard enters into many of the petty worries and annoyances that had to be borne. One long-handled broom had "to do duty for sweeping among half-a-dozen families, and getting the broom early in the morning was a luxury." Numbers crowded round the fire in the kitchen every hour of the day, and it sometimes happened that "what one cooked another annexed." Mistress and maid had to sleep in the same apartment, and not a few were without maids or any one else to help. These are, however, incidents inseparable from such conditions as those under which we were now placed. They were little noticed at the time, and are of no interest to any one now; not even to those whom circumstances compelled to live in such close proximity to one another.

It would but weary the reader to enter into the routine of daily life during the next few months. Those of us who had the care and responsibility of the place on our shoulders knew little rest by day or by night. Sentries were nightly posted round the encampment to guard against possible surprise, and what was even more important, to prevent theft. Their instructions among other things were, that any messengers arriving were to be conducted to the window of my room, and this led to awkward mistakes, of which the following is an illustration. A messenger arrived with a letter one morning about 2 A.M., and was directed to my window, but not understanding his instructions, went to the next one to it, and tapped. Being answered from within he called out "a letter." The occupants of the room thought he was calling for a ladder, and that the place must be on fire, went into the corridor and screamed loudly and repeatedly. I at once rushed out to see what was amiss, and found naked figures pouring from every door, screaming and moaning as if ten thousand Gcalekas were upon us. After a measure of silence was obtained, our friend told her story and was ordered back to bed. This is but one of many such alarms, all of them equally silly, and most of them excessively irritating to those who could only snatch a few hours' sleep at odd intervals.

We made what efforts we could to entertain our guests. Concerts, lectures, readings, and recitations were arranged, and did something to relieve the dull monotony of waiting for news from the scene of strife. On one occasion I made a rather unfortunate selection. I read Poe's "Raven," and the result was anything but encouraging. During the night the concert, or cheese, induced nightmare, and more than one lady alarmed us all by uttering piercing screams, which resounded through the building, and brought people trooping into the corridors to hear whether the enemy had actually taken the fort. The same night a "doughty warrior" was found at his tent door slashing at imaginary enemies with his riding whip in lieu of a claymore or battle-axe.

The Rev. Mr. Leslie was one of the refugees. He had lived among the Gcalekas for a number of years, and had done excellent work at his station of Tetura. Personally he was very popular among them, and at the outbreak of hostilities they neither burned his house nor church. After the troops had taken possession of the district in which his station was situated, he paid it a visit along with one or two other friends. Though the Gcalekas neither interfered with house nor furniture, there was one thing to which they turned their most serious attention, and that was a quantity of drugs they found about his library. Leslie knew something of pharmacy, and kept a well stored medicine chest, of which he made daily use in connection with his missionary work. When the Gcaleka army found themselves in possession of this treasure, the great war doctor was consulted as to what they should do with it. He, after much deliberation, hit upon the following excellent plan, and proceeded to act upon it. All powders and dry substances, from chalk to calomel, and from simple ointment to cantharides, he mixed together in a large basin, and having taken a sufficiency of castor oil from a stock bottle, he made the whole into one mass, which being thoroughly mixed together, and charms added, was set aside for a night. The liquids contained in bottles, and which included such substances as sulphuric acid and aconite, he treated in a similar manner. On the following morning he dosed the regiment, giving each brave draught or bolus according to his particular fancy. The results were more startling than satisfactory. During the whole of that day and the succeeding night, men lay groaning as in the last agonies of sea-sickness. Others in a frenzy of pain ran they knew not whither. The doctor was at his wits' end, while the generals concluded that "white man's drugs are of no use as war medicine." When the matter was reported to Kreli he disgraced the doctor, but as N'qeto was a general favourite he still retained much influence. After the war he lived for years in nominal hiding, but really in a kind of honourable retirement.

The tedious course of the campaign it is not my business to follow. Every week brought fresh complications. The Gaikas were disaffected, and one Commissioner after another was sent to negotiate, but to little purpose. At last the Hon. C. Brownlee went to see Sandili, and as Kreli a few months before had called his attention to the length of his "tail," so Sandili closed the conference by throwing his whip on the ground saying, " Chalis, there is a puff adder, and if you tramp upon it, it will bite you." " Chalis" took the hint and did not continue to urge his views. Among our casual visitors at Blythswood was the Rev. James Davidson of Mbulu, who had manfully stuck to his station, and who with his wife and family came to spend a few days at Blythswood. Their visit I enjoyed more than any episode during the war, but even such friendly visits in the excited state of feeling prevailing created difficulties. Mr. Davidson's waggon driver was a Fingoe, and when in camp said somewhat unguardedly that at the Gwadana fight the " police had bolted." This they had actually done, and that in every direction, and very rightly too. But then, of our gallant fifteen more than half were Gwadana heroes, and being insulted by such sinister accusations, they laid violent hands on the Fingoe, and before I knew of the stir, tried and sentenced him to twelve lashes with a stirrup leather, which were duly administered. The man immediately came to me to lodge a complaint, and I naturally felt that if all civil authority was to be thus usurped, there was an end of order. So measures were taken by which our gallant fifteen found other fields for the exercise of their gifts, and we did not lament their loss nearly as much as we ought to have done from their point of view. Reorganisation and more effective discipline in after years, converted the moribund Frontier Mounted Police into the smart and active Cape Mounted Rifles.

My neighbour missionary, the Rev. Richard Ross of Cunningham, like Mr. Davidson of Mbulu, had stuck to his guns and remained at his station. For both it was a time of great anxiety, but they felt that their remaining would do much to give their people confidence, and in some measure stop the panic among loyals. Mr. Davidson's station was in close proximity to the Gaika and Tembu borders, and an outbreak from either quarter might bring hostile forces down upon them in a single night. In these trying circumstances he remained at his post, and so far as practicable, continued his ordinary work.

Mr. Ross was placed in peculiarly difficult circumstances. His station lies in the direct line of communication between Gcalekaland and Gaika country, and parties from either army, passing and repassing, would take it in their line of march. For days, weeks, months, this state of anxiety continued. At intervals he was able to save small fugitive parties of rebels, wishing to surrender, from the vengeance of the Fingoes. Gaikas from the Colony, who knew him as a boy, came for advice, and found in him a wise counsellor in the day of their perplexity. The strain, however, was very great, and such as could hardly fail to tell upon the health of any man, and to the anxieties of this time, in part at least, must have been due the breakdown of his health which happened a few years later.

Living with Mr. Ross's family at this time was a young English lady, who, towards the end of December, was most anxious to visit friends at Queen's Town. The threatening attitude of the Tembu tribes made travelling between the Transkei and Queen's Town very unsafe, and for weeks no one unprotected by a strong escort had attempted the journey. At this very time I was anxious to proceed to England, and as Mr. Ross could not leave his home for any length of time, I volunteered to take Miss Houldsworth to Queen's Town.

Acting on this arrangement, I placed Blythswood in temporary charge of Mr. Thomas Brown, and left for Queen's Town on a Monday morning about an hour before dawn. That same evening we arrived at Southey Ville, a remote station where a Mr. Levy was Resident with a tribe of Tembus. There we found both Mr. Levy and the Fingoe Resident, Mr. Ayliff, who had gone up to give his brother officer such moral support as he could in most difficult and critical circumstances. Both regarded the road to Queen's Town as unsafe and the risks too great to be undertaken. The final decision as to proceeding or returning was left till the following day, but we all felt as if the course to be pursued was a foregone conclusion.

During the night scouts brought in favourable reports, and long before dawn Mr. Levy came to my room to say he thought we might venture to go forward, as the main body of the Tembu army had gone to another and distant part of the country, and that for the time their whole attention would be centered on that part. With the first streaks of light we started under escort of six mounted police to protect us from molestation at disaffected villages we had to pass on our way. The first part of the journey was the most dangerous. Our way lay through rugged mountain passes—the home of marauders and robbers. About ten miles from Southey Ville we had to pass through a narrow defile between two very steep mountains, with a winding road scarped out of the hill-side close to the edge of a wild mountain torrent. Just as we were about to enter the pass, I heard a most unearthly yelling, as if Pandemonium were set loose, away down the gorge. I stopped to listen, and at once detected, in the pauses between the yells, the trampling of horses at a gallop. I had time to turn the horses' heads, and leave the whole width of the road clear before the cause of all the din came in sight. As I turned out of the road the policemen closed up and involuntarily cocked their carbines. I ordered them on no account to fire except in the last extremity. My companion sat beside me as still as a statue. Nearer came the tramping, and louder became the shouts of the savage riders. It was a moment of intense anxiety. Presently a troop of horses, some with halters, others with the long mane and tail of the unbroken colt, swept round the curve of an intervening rock. After these came a party of eight or ten mounted men riding as if for life. They passed us like a whirlwind, and in less time than it takes to write the words disappeared in a cloud of dust. We could hear their whoops and the loud clap of their stock whips long after we lost sight of them. Whether they even saw us I do not know; in any case they represented nothing more formidable than a party of stock thieves who had made a successful raid on some luckless farmer during the preceding night, and who were now returning to their native fastnesses with the spoil.

We continued our journey, and without further interruption arrived at Queen's Town, glad to return to civilisation and leave the dangers of running the gauntlet through the enemy's country behind. I had, however, to solve the problem of how to return to King William's Town and the coast. Between my leaving Blythswood and my arrival in Queen's Town the Gaikas had assumed an attitude which made it impossible to travel through their country. I had no alternative but to make a detour of a hundred miles, through country deserted by the inhabitants and presenting a most dreary and forsaken aspect, to reach Fort Beaufort, and thence Lovedale. From Queen's Town I had taken a lady who had for days waited for an opportunity of travelling down country. As we proceeded on our journey it became apparent that we could get no better accommodation than a deserted outhouse for the night. At one farm house we saw a lovely Persian cat and some fowls, but during the whole day met with no other sign of human occupation.

We arrived at night at a farm on the northern slope of the Amatola range of mountains. Here we found a Hottentot servant in charge—the family, like others, had gone to a place of safety with their flocks and herds. He made a grand fire in the kitchen, and having plenty of provisions we were soon seated partaking of a hearty supper of mutton chops, bread and coffee. The rooms of the house were locked, but a plentiful supply of straw laid on the earthen floor of the kitchen, made, with the aid of our rugs, an excellent bed, and we slept none the less soundly because of our novel surroundings, and the somewhat unusual arrangement of each in a corner huddled up in rugs and straw. The next day we reached Lovedale, and after resting my sorely jaded horses I made my way by easy stages to King William's Town and the coast.

That same week I sailed for England, and left the war to drag its length of weary months slowly along. Before my return, twelve months later, much history had been made, and the whole face of Kaffraria for ever changed.

I left Cape Town during the sweltering heat of summer, and arrived at Plymouth on the 22nd of January in a hurricane of snow. Two days later I presented myself at the offices of the Mission in Edinburgh, and got anything but a cordial welcome. When I entered the room the man of office first rose from his seat; next he sat down, removed his glasses and eyed me up and down and all over. At last he found voice, and said in his severest manner, "You here!" I felt it would not do to laugh, so I came promptly to the relief of his perplexity by explaining that my visit to Scotland was to be very brief, and that I did not intend to return alone. Being thus mollified the frown cleared away, and the troubled waters were immediately smooth. I had arranged to return in two months, but ten weary moons came and went before a return to the Transkei became feasible, and even then, as the event proved, we were but at the beginning of South African troubles.

* * * *

We returned to Blythswood on the 29th January, 1879, and it was decided to have a second opening on the 2nd of February. When we left England, South Africa was reported to be fully pacified. By the time we reached Cape Town, the Zulu war had begun, and troops were being hurried Natalward. On the 1st of February we knew of the disaster which had befallen Lord Chelmsford's ill-starred expedition, that is to say, we knew it through native report at a distance of 500 miles, and only three days after the first telegraphic intelligence had reached us. At the meeting on the 2nd, the Fingoes readily voted money to clear off what debt remained on Blythswood, and expressed their willingness to help the Institution in every way. But when the chief magistrate proposed that they should express their willingness to go to fight in Zululand if called upon, the younger men stood up, but all the old men thought they had parted with their senses. The memory of the devastations of Tshaka, when ruler of Zululand, caused a thrill of fear to pass through all South Africa. The natives felt persuaded that his successor would serve the English, as he had all his neighbours, and that at last the white man had met a foe before whom he would be weak as other men.

The troubles which began on the Tugela during the first days of 1879 kept South-East Africa in a ferment till 1882.

The year 1879 was one of comparative peace and progress in the Transkei. The Zulu war dragged its weary length over many a blood-stained field, but though we heard of the din of battle and the clash of arms, we were too far removed from the actual scene of strife to be very greatly disturbed after the first panic had passed away.

My first care after the re-opening of Blythswood was to organise the trades' departments which it was resolved should be added to the Institution. This required time, care, and extreme caution, the more especially as the industrial departments were expected to be from the first self-supporting. Both present and future success depended on our being able to turn out good work—to keep our promises as regarded time, and sell at rates not higher than ordinary jobbers whose work was much inferior to what we produced.

I was fortunate in having an excellent foreman, Thomas Brown, who still occupies the same position, and is a man of the most sterling integrity. He had both energy and perseverance in any work he undertook, and what was of perhaps greater value, he made the interests of the Institution his own. Under his careful management the industries prospered, and at the end of his first financial year he was able to show the very handsome balance of £163, after making full allowance for rent, tear and wear of tools, depreciation of stock, and all other incidental losses. This, so far as I am aware, is the only instance in South Africa of Mission industries being financially successful from the first.

There were other matters which claimed immediate attention as well as our industries. During the occupation of the previous year by refugees, vast quantities of rubbish had accumulated, and the unsightly mounds of earth, thrown up hastily for defence, remained *in situ*. To remove these, level the ground, fill up old rifle pits, make paths through the rough and tangled grass, and plant a few trees and shrubs, kept me much occupied out-of-doors during the first six months of the year. The question of our water supply was also a source of perplexity. A water race had been cut shortly after the commencement of the building, but the survey having been made during the rainy season, and by a man who was a stranger in the district, it was afterwards found that the "strong fountain," from which the supply came, was, in dry weather, neither better nor worse than a hard, sun-baked clay pit. The furrow, over a mile long, had to be cut afresh from a point about 200 yards lower down the valley. The surveying for it, as well as the levelling, I had to do myself, there being no professional surveyor in the district. Most of the labour was done by the pupils during the two hours' afternoon work they all are expected to do.

During the first year the numbers in attendance were, fifty-seven school pupils and fifteen trades apprentices; and when the unsettled condition of the country generally is taken into account, their diligence and progress were extremely satisfactory. I cannot sum up the year's efforts better than by transcribing a few sentences from the first report made by H.M. Inspector of Schools. Mr. Clark, in his report, after giving the tabulative classification of the pupils, says:—

"*Industrial Department.*—In this department, in aid of which an annual grant of £120 is received from Government, there is as yet but one trade being carried on—viz., carpentry. The master carpenter, Mr. Brown, has under him thirteen apprentices, of whose docility and industry he speaks very highly. These apprentices are taught carpentry of every description, and several of them are already so advanced in the knowledge of their trade, that sundry articles of domestic furniture made by them and exhibited

G

at the Transkei Agricultural Show in May last, were awarded prizes. The workshops, although so to speak temporary, are moderately roomy and convenient, and I am informed that the department is never at a standstill for want of work; on the contrary, the master carpenter tells me that he receives orders for various kinds of work faster than he can execute them. I am permitted by the Rev. J. Macdonald, the Head-master of the Institution, to state that the total value of the work done in the trade department since its commencement (October, 1879) is £1484. This sum includes the cost of material used, and Mr. Macdonald adds that, though the amount seems considerable, the actual profits have been but very moderate. From what I saw and learned of the working of Mr. Brown's branch of the Institution, I am convinced that a good work is being done. The beneficial effects of native youths being taught handicrafts can hardly be over-estimated, and the industrial department of Blythswood, though as yet in its infancy, supplies a want long felt in the Transkei district.

"*Sewing School.*—Teacher, Lizzie Mabentsela. On the books, twenty-two girls, present fifteen girls. The more advanced of the pupils in this class are able to cut out and make up dresses and other articles of wearing apparel, while the small children do plain sewing of a simple kind. The first prize for the best made dress at the Transkei Show, in May last, was awarded to a girl from Blythswood, who attends this class, and whose needlework was much commended for its neatness and excellence. The sewing school is under the immediate and personal superintendence of Mrs. Macdonald, who reports most favourably of the progress and industry of the children.

"*Boarding Department.*—There are at present in this department of the Institution fifty-six boarders, including the thirteen apprentices. The accommodation is most ample, and leaves nothing to be desired on the score of either sanitary arrangements or convenience. The Institution itself, which is a handsome stone building, two storeys high, measuring 200 feet by 36 feet, was built with a view to the accommodation of boarders, and contains twenty-one dormitories, of which thirteen are intended for natives, and are well capable of accommodating 104 pupils, while the remaining eight are intended for the accommodation of twenty-four European boarders. In addition to those dormitories, and the hall already mentioned above, the building contains the head-master's wing, library, teachers' rooms, &c., with all the necessary offices of such an establishment. There is also an unfinished portion of the building, intended for class-rooms, which, when completed, will give four rooms of 26 feet by 16 feet each.

"*General Remarks.*—Blythswood Institution has from the first led a somewhat chequered existence, having done duty as a fort and harbour of refuge during the Gcaleka war of 1877-78, and only really commenced work in February, 1879. Giving due consideration, therefore, to the difficulties it has had to contend with, and the very recent date of its opening, I consider the results it has already produced most satisfactory and promising. The state of the classes, as regards discipline and organisation, is excellent; and I have every reason to be gratified at the condition in which I found the several branches of the Institution. The standard of work is doubtless lower than what would naturally be looked for in an educational establishment of its pretensions, but when the very low standard of the majority of the schools from which Blythswood is recruited is taken into consideration, and due allowance is made for the uphill work attending the floating of a large training school such as this, it would, I think, be most unreasonable and unjust to expect that more could have been done in the time.—(Signed) CHARLES CLARK, Inspector of Schools."

Not long after Mr. Clark had paid his visit of inspection, we had another visitor, whose observations of missionary work among the Kaffirs were published in the Edinburgh *Daily Review*. A notice of Blythswood appeared on the 29th of October, 1880, and from it I extract the following paragraphs :—

"Most readers of the *Review* are more or less familiar with the circumstances under which the Free Church Institution at Blythswood was erected. We do not often hear of natives contributing thousands of pounds for educational purposes, but this the Fingoes did. From first to last they have contributed over £4000 for the erection of a school for the education of their children. Various notices of the progress of the work have at different times appeared, written chiefly by the missionaries on the spot, but I am not aware of any report by an unprejudiced layman having hitherto been published.

"Missionaries are frequently accused of giving their reports a rosy tint with the view of influencing contributions from the home churches. I am not prepared to say in how far the accusation may be just. No doubt some missionaries have exaggerated, but it is equally certain others have undervalued their work and its results, probably through fear of laying themselves open to the reproach of having painted an overdrawn picture of Christian work. No such accusation can, however, be charged against Government Inspectors of Schools. They have established a name for themselves, for ability, fairness, and soundness of judgment, which has only gathered volume with the lapse of years.

"Blythswood being in receipt of Government aid, is

subject to inspection, and Mr. Charles Clark paid it his first official visit in June last. His report, as published in the Education Blue-book, is very full, and is made up with great care and accuracy. The pupils are classified according to the various standards of education at the Cape, and each is set down in his proper place. The order, teaching, and general working arrangements carried out by the Rev. J. Macdonald, the principal, are commended in the highest terms, while many of the pupils are said to have done the various exercises set with ease and accuracy."

VI.

FRESH TROUBLES—BURNED HOMESTEADS AND RUINED MISSIONS.

THE moons came and went swiftly, and we were gradually getting the Mission at Blythswood into form and order. Our time was very fully occupied, and we found the work both pleasant and interesting. It seemed as if at last the Institution had emerged from its initial difficulties, and had finally entered upon its work of education and civilisation. There were, however, events transpiring in the territories to the north and east of us which affected Blythswood, and altered the whole conditions of Tembuland and East Griqualand to the borders of Natal. These made the development of the Mission in that direction necessary. To understand the events referred to we must go back a few months.

At the close of the Gcaleka war the Government of the Cape Colony passed a Disarming Act, to apply not only within the Colony, but to all territories under its jurisdiction, from Natal on the one hand to the Dutch Republic on the other. This Act affected a large number of semi-independent and warlike tribes, and was keenly resented by them. This was bad enough, but when to it was added the insane policy of disarming the loyal Fingoes and tribes within the Colony before taking any effectual steps to secure their safety or disarm the disaffected, it needed no special insight into native character to predict trouble in the near future. The arms surrendered by the loyals were, after being valued and paid for, burned. The intention was good; the results disastrous. Government meant to show that it put no value upon the weapons; it actually did show to the large disaffected tribes an unprotected and open road by which they could advance upon and attack the Colony.

The Fingoes being disarmed, the Government next turned its attention to the Basutos. Of all the tribes under its rule the Basutos were one of the most progressive in the arts of industry and civilisation. In a very few years they had converted the valleys of their highland country into well tilled farms and smiling orchards. Water races to irrigate their crops were constructed by the hundred, and many of them had discarded the "bee-hive" for good stone or brick houses containing several apartments. Christian Missions had succeeded beyond the most sanguine expectations, and the native converts had made an effort to support a station among the Barotsi in the basin of the distant Zambesi. They had come under Colonial rule as an unbroken and independent tribe, to whom certain national rights were secured by treaty. The Disarming Act they regarded as an infringement of their treaty rights, and they resolved to resist it to the utmost of their power. There was no disorder and no raids into other territories; they simply took up a position of passive resistance. The Government was determined to enforce its policy, and pushed matters to extremities by sending an army of occupation to Basutoland. With the Basutos all the disaffected tribes sympathised. The Pondos gave pledges of active support, but ultimately held back to see how the fortunes of war were to turn. The Pondomise under Umhlonhlo and Umditshwa threw off the mask and went into open revolt. The former of these, while professing ardent loyalty, and offering his services against the Basutos, murdered the local Magistrate and his staff in cold blood. He had called a great muster of his warriors, professedly to march against the Basutos, but in reality in order to throw the English officers off their guard and lure them to their doom. The Tembus, upon our borders, were disaffected and were anxious at once to support the Basutos, and wipe out old scores with the disarmed Fingoes.

For weeks I had been hearing sinister rumours from beyond the border, and in order to satisfy myself sent one of my native teachers, in the guise of a rebel, on a journey through a great part of Tembuland. This man had every qualification that could favour him in the part he was to act as a spy. He was a

Gaika by race and was related to some well-known rebels in the Gcaleka disturbance. By marriage he was connected with the chief Dukwana, who, Christian and Presbyterian elder as he was, cast in his lot with his countrymen and fell fighting for native independence. It was his head that was carried in a pocket-handkerchief to headquarters by Mr. ——, a Colonial officer, and then—— but I had better not proceed. Deeds done during war belong to a category of their own, and it is better that many of them should not be repeated. When the *radius* and *ulna*, removed from the arm of a great chief "for scientific purposes," are converted into riding whip handles, and shown to all and sundry as a curiosity, we get a glimpse of the evil side of human nature more instructive than pages of description as to the process by which human skulls can be made into flower pots or drinking cups.

My messenger was well received and taken into confidence by several men of high standing among the Tembus, and on his return I felt I could rely on the accuracy of his information. From facts which he was able to ascertain, it needed no prophet to foretell what was likely to transpire within the next few weeks. I could not divulge my information in detail for the very good reason that I could prove nothing. I did, however, write to a high, very high officer, giving such information as I possessed in general terms, and received from him the ordinary official, "I have the honour to acknowledge receipt of your courtesy, &c., ending with a sting in its tail, and a hint to mind my own business and not turn alarmist; the Government were fully informed through their officers of all that was transpiring in Tembuland." The event speedily proved the precise value to be attached to the information received through their officers.

The crisis came. Things drifted from bad to worse till, suddenly and unexpectedly, the whole country was in a blaze, and no preparation made to meet it. Without note or warning, Hope was murdered by his own people. Welsh, at Tsolo, was shut up in his own gaol, with a few others, who found a precarious refuge there; Thomson was beleaguered in Chevi Chase; Cumming, at Maclear; while Stanford, Leifeldt, Brownlee, and others, saved their lives by flight. The whole country was on the war path, and the disarmed Fingoes were an easy prey. In the Transkei the Government had neither arms nor ammunition. Major Elliott telegraphed from Umtata to Pattle, at Idutywa, for ammunition, and the latter replied that he had only eighteen rounds at his office. The whole police force was in Basutoland, and every soldier fit for duty was in Zululand. Such was the state of preparation when my second experience of war began. I had no sense of fear, but my heart sank within me as I, for the second time, within so short a period, contemplated the utter demolition of all I had done, and upon which I had expended so much thought and toil. I seemed to look into the blackness of a tempestuous night.

For a week after this, things were in a most critical condition. Raids were made on every hand, and many men lost their lives. Two or three times the enemy advanced far into Fingoland, pillaging and burning at leisure. We had resolved to remain at Blythswood to the last; and the last seemed to have come. For three nights, my wife's and my own horses stood saddled in the stable, to be ready in case of emergency. Once only did a false alarm disturb us much. It was caused by one of our own people, who mistook a party of stock thieves for the advance guard of a Tembu army. The error was discovered almost immediately, so we did not even arouse the pupils. The Fingoes during this time were in a state of hopeless panic. They had seen their arms burned a few weeks before the outbreak, and now the Government did not seem able to help them, or redeem its own promises. Fortunately, divided councils among the Tembu chiefs, and waiting for other tribes to join in the rebellion, caused them to delay making any serious incursions. By the time they had their plans matured troops had arrived, and the passes were securely guarded. Attempts were made to force them, but little damage was done, and within two months of the first revolt, the war, so far as Tembuland was concerned, became a huge cattle drive. Not so Basutoland and East Griqualand; but to these provinces I shall refer in another place.

At Blythswood we continued our work, so far as that could be done, and were able to give shelter to a few homeless families from the borders. Of the Europeans in Tembuland, most had fled to Queen's Town. But in both East Griqualand and Tembuland, many were unable to leave the territories. Of these several lost their lives, others escaped as if by miracle, while some were most kindly treated by the rebels.

Mention has already been made of Mr. Welsh as being shut up, with a few others, and besieged in his own gaol. The following details of their imprisonment, told to the writer by his daughter, and written down at the time, is not devoid of interest, even after the lapse of so many years. Miss Welsh said :—

"On the afternoon of Saturday we first heard of the murder of Mr. Hope, at Sulenkama, and knew that any attempt to escape out of the territory would be hopeless. We got the native constables and one or two more together, and began to remove all our provisions and bedding to the gaol. Notice was sent of what had happened to all Europeans within reach.

"At dusk we all went into the gaol. When the whole were gathered together, there were thirty-four persons, including the children and blacks, packed into a building only twenty-five feet long by about seventeen feet wide. The building was divided into two rooms, without a door between, and a small hole dug out of the brickwork served for an intermediate door. We could seldom get out all the time we were there, and the closeness was, at times, dreadful.

"On Sunday morning a number of rebels came and drove away our cattle and horses. One of our policemen, when he saw his horse taken away got very excited, and wanted to fire at the man. Some one took his gun from him, but he was a long while before he got quieted down, as he had been very fond of his horse. A young man who was friendly came near, and told us the people meant mischief, that we must be on our guard, and not trust ourselves to them whatever promise they made.

"The 'warriors' wanted a palaver, and papa went outside to talk to them. For two hours he sat on a stone, with a wild warrior, holding a spear in his hand, sitting opposite him. Mamma had gone outside and sat near the door, and Mr. Cumming was there too, watching every movement among the crowd, to be sure that none of them came round behind to get at the door. This was the most dangerous position we were in all along, but both papa and Mr. Cumming thought we must show them we were not afraid, and that they would not be so apt to attack us. After the palaver was finished we went inside, and the rebels sat in a group at a distance, discussing what was to be done, and how they could get us out. Before sunset they dispersed, and another night passed quietly.

"On Monday, the chief with a select party of councillors and a long train of warriors came to the Residency to say they wanted to see the Magistrate. There was a very long conference, but none of us went outside. The chief urged very strongly that we should leave to go to Umtata. This proposal was rejected, and excuses made to gain time. We discovered, afterwards, that they had decided to kill the whole party four miles on the road to Umtata, if we had consented to leave.

"On Tuesday morning, one of the great councillors sent us a live sheep as food. This surprised us, but we found afterwards that it had been 'doctored' by the magicians so that on eating of it we should leave our shelter and be at their mercy. We eat the sheep, but the medicine did not act. 'It was not strong enough.'

"There was one man who was most kind to us. One evening he came pretending to look about, and when near enough said, 'How are you off for food? I shall try to send you some to-night.' Being asked if he could send a message to Umtata, he said, 'No, I am watched.' At midnight he came again, bringing half-a-sheep and a bucket of milk, and, at the same time, undertook the dangerous duty of seeing a letter to Umtata.

"We had many curious experiences in the gaol, there being so many of us crowded into such little space. We even joked now and then, and the people teased papa about his sending others to prison, and said he would have more sympathy with rogues after his own experience of prison life. One night, our cook was lying asleep before a large fire. Some one went for hot water, and spilled a little of it on him. He thought it was a rebel's spear, and got up yelling and shouting, 'I am dead.' One day, a report was started that our food supply was getting very low. Our only stout gentleman got quite alarmed, and amused us all immensely. We had very few dishes and no tables, so we all had our food in relays on the floor. At first, we were so much afraid of our water supply being cut off that water for washing dishes was measured out almost in wine-glassfuls, certainly in tea-cupfuls. A very stout lady of the party was greatly distressed at being seen going through the small hole in our intermediate wall. This was all the more comical, as we had to do so many things of a more distressing character in a semi-public manner, but somehow our friend could not get over the idea of being seen squeezing through the narrow opening.

"From the gaol windows, we could see the office and our own house. The natives during the first four days took away every thing they could carry. Their first great find was the office safe, but, after spending nearly a day hammering at it to force it open, they found it empty. They got a lot of office papers and books, and sat under the verandah holding mock trials. One man got a big family Bible, and sat down solemnly as if to conduct a religious service. They carried the piano outside and opened it. One of them touched the keys, and literally jumped into the air. After his first fright, he viewed it from a distance of ten or fifteen yards, and unslinging his rifle fired at the offending instrument. It could now do no further harm, and he walked boldly up to it, to get a second surprise and a bigger fright than at the first. After this the piano was left alone for that day.

"When the relief party arrived, we were ordered to leave at once. We had to leave clothes, books, jewels, plate, everything, for the Pondos. They soon ransacked our boxes, and it was most amusing to see the lucky braves marching along. Several of them were dressed in our spare petticoats, others in print dresses. One wore a gaudy coloured tea-cosey as a helmet, his sole garment; another extemporised a scarlet tunic out of a lady's undergarment, and one sailed about in a white satin skirt of mine with very full train. To see him, as he tried to manage that to him unwieldy train, was a study which one can never forget.

"At last we got fairly under way, and after a most anxious night, spent at Gongululu, we arrived at Umtata in safety. Father all along suspected Pondo treachery, and, in the end, it was discovered that they had arranged that, before we were allowed to enter the village, a quarrel should be picked and that they should keep their compact with the rebels by murdering papa and Mr. Cumming. A whisper of this had reached Umtata, and steps were taken to circumvent their designs."

Such are the dangers to which those occupying distant posts are at times exposed.

The school session at Blythswood closed late in December. The previous months had been a time of deep anxiety to all living beyond the frontier, and of danger to many. As the war cloud began to lift once more, the missionaries returned to their stations. That is to their stations, but not to their homes and Missions. Many of their churches and dwellings were in ashes, and their people scattered or dead. Half the Missions beyond the frontier were a ruin and a desolation, and the work was not so much re-organisation as the creation of new centres.

We all felt that the work before us must involve great physical toil and extreme caution, if the new departure was to be on a permanent basis. The re-organisation and development of the work in Tembuland and East Griqualand was intrusted to the Rev. Richard Ross and myself, and this arrangement made heavy calls on one's time and strength. When just entering on these duties, and anxious to master all the details by a personal inspection of the respective districts, I was suddenly interrupted in my work. On the 15th of February I had occasion to go to Ibeka, a distance of twenty-five miles. We were returning late at night with a bright moon shining. Our four horses were going at a good round pace, when suddenly the leaders shied, and the wheels having come against some obstruction, I was thrown out. In falling I got entangled for a second between the wheel and the step, and presently found myself lying on the ground with a dislocated ankle and a broken *fibula*.

I was lifted on to my own saddle horse, which was being led, and rode to the Idutywa Residency, about a mile distant from where the accident happened. The next ten weeks gave me an opportunity to rest and—grumble. It was most provoking to be confined to bed at this particular time, but there was no help for it, and I spent my time between reading and fretting as best I could. My recovery was slow, unsatisfactory, and tedious. It was not till the end of the year I felt quite fit for work, and even then the limb often ached if I sat long on horseback.

VII.

JOURNEYS AND EXTENDED MISSIONARY OPERATIONS.

DURING 1881 circumstances prevented much being done in the region to the north-east of us, but in November Mr. Ross paid a visit to East Griqualand. Two days after his return he was struck down with a painful illness, from which he did not recover for nearly three years, and the whole work of reconstruction fell upon me, as well as the care of his station of Cunningham. Duff was my head-quarters, but I made a monthly visit to Cunningham, a distance of forty-five miles, and a quarterly visit to East Griqualand, a distance of about 140 miles in a direct line, but involving, each journey, a ride of over 300 miles. My first visit there was made in 1882.

At noon on the 19th of April I started from Idutywa for Qumbu and Gatberg, accompanied by one of the elders of the district, my groom, and a native interpreter. My equipment consisted simply of sleeping rugs and waterproof coats. I carried neither provisions nor camping paraphernalia, and had only one spare horse, in case of accident to those we rode. The day was excessively hot, and progress correspondingly slow. We managed to reach Umtēntū, thirty miles distant, shortly after dusk, having made a fair beginning with " incidents of the journey " at the Bashee, in which I had a dip through my horse becoming restive in the middle of the river. The following day we reached Umtata. This village boasts a cathedral, and is an Episcopal See.

On Friday, the 21st, we travelled the greater portion of the day through Pondoland. To the north-east of our line of march lay the great mountain chain separating this fairest of South African Provinces from the territory where the recent revolt originated. To the south and south-east illimitable plains and undulations of hill and dale stretched away to the distant ocean. This vast territory, one or two Mission stations excepted, is one mass of heathenism, where all its obscene and barbarously cruel practices flourish in undisguised publicity; where the lightning-man dupes hundreds of the credulous to part with their substance to secure immunity from the thunderbolt; where the witch-doctor follows his devilish craft, and dooms the innocent to death to preserve his own reputation; where the most depraved scoundrels, European and African, find a secure retreat from law and justice; and where, in short, no man's life is worth a day's purchase. One must see the difference between tribes under British rule and those who are independent, to realise the advantages of the former over the latter. The actual condition of every-day life and the theories wrought out in snug studies or at drawing-room parties differ in nothing more than they do in this, and any one visiting South Africa finds a speedy death-blow given to many cherished theories.

Towards evening of this day we reached Qumbu as the sun was setting in a turbulent sky of deepest red, a sure sign that the first stage of our journey was completed just in time. The Magistrate, Mr. Brownlee, was absent, but I found comfortable quarters at an "accommodation house" kept by a Scotchman named M'Glashan. The following morning the Scripture-reader from Gatberg, accompanied by an elder resident at Qumbu and a number of Christian people, came to meet me. They expressed the greatest delight at seeing me amongst them.

During one of the many interviews I had with the principal men, they told me the story of their escape during the rebellion, and it is characteristic of the dangers of that unhappy period. "The first we heard of actual revolt was after Magyi at Mataticle was openly in arms against the Government. Then Mr. Hope, our Magistrate, called us, and intimated to us—Christian people—that war had commenced at Mataticle. Mr. Hope was anxious to march at once, but Umhlonhlo said he must wait a full muster of the tribe. This he did, and marched when the muster was complete. Shortly thereafter a man came to the Residency and reported that he had heard the

Pondomisi say they meant to murder Mr. Hope, and that he believed it to be true. Ntame, who was in charge of the men at the Residency, sent a note to Mr. Hope warning him of his danger, but he replied, 'Tell the people I am drinking [friendly] with Umhlonhlo and his people.' The following day, at a war-dance given professedly in his honour, he was murdered by order of Umhlonhlo. The news spread like wildfire through the country, and filled the few loyals at the Residency with consternation. Next day the Pondomisi assembled in thousands, and they were then placed inside a ring of warriors, while their fate was being discussed in council. After a long discussion it was resolved to spare their lives, and they were ordered to return to their homes. A few days thereafter, still fearing they might be put to death, they sent a messenger to Mr. Blenkins, who was advancing from Kokstad by forced marches to the relief of Mr. Welsh, who was known to be shut up with a few others in his own gaol. Mr. Blenkins promised to relieve them as he passed through the district. By some accident the Pondomisi suspected that communications had passed between the loyals and the Government people elsewhere, and they resolved to spare them no longer. Mr. Blenkins was meantime unable to ford the Tina, owing to continued heavy rains. When matters were thus becoming desperate, the loyals determined to leave the sick and aged behind and flee in the night. In this they succeeded, but the Pondomisi vented their rage and disappointment on the aged and bedridden, who were ruthlessly butchered."

The following day being Sunday the sacrament of the Lord's Supper was dispensed, when twenty-six persons sat down at the table. The services were conducted in a large circular hut, which was suitably fitted up for the occasion. The audience numbered over 120, and those unable to obtain admission sat round the door outside.

This was the first occasion on which the sacraments were dispensed, in that vast territory, after the Presbyterian form.

On Monday I visited the famous falls of the Tsitsa. Above the falls the river flows placidly through open country with arable land on either side down to the water's edge. It then takes a sudden bound of over 300 feet sheer down without a break in the face of the stupendous cliff, and then flows for many miles through one of the wildest gorges conceivable.

The waterfall itself it is impossible to describe adequately. The river where it takes this magnificent bound is about three times the size of the Clyde at Lanark, and the water as it flows over the edge, first bends down unbroken in "pure polished velocity." The motion is so swift and smooth that the eye cannot follow it, except when a foam globe from above darts over it, and sends back a flash of mingled colours. Just underneath the edge, the smooth flowing water breaks into foam and furrows, which, in the strong light of the sun, burn like 10,000 crystal candelabra, polished with more than earthly splendour.

Ever and anon a great jet of water, bursting out, startles one with its flash of pure white light, presently vanishing in lightest spray and gossamer cloud. The water as it descends gathers in mid air into huge masses, which, crashing and bursting on the surface of the seething caldron below, give a succession of reports resembling, when heard at a distance, the almost simultaneous discharge of an immense number of heavy guns. When one is close by, the roar is continuous and perfectly deafening, while showers of spray rise hundreds of feet till lost in the blue haze. A perpetual iris encircles the lower portion of the fall, forming arcs of colour so varied in form and so changeable in colour as to mock the keenest sighted eye.

The river below the fall, as seen from the high banks, is a most imposing sight. High precipitous rocks; giant columns of blackest basalt; veins of dazzling brightness; water pools of deepest green; snow white cascades and foliage of every hue and tint at once surprise and delight the beholder. Above all is the sense of rugged strength and eternal stability, which this noble river with its magnificent cataract, leaves indelibly written on the mind of him who once sees it and drinks in its awful grandeur.

After visiting this wild and romantic spot we returned to Qumbu, by way of the Wesleyan Institution for Girls at Shawbury. This is one of the few spots, in that far away land, from which a pure stream of light emanates. For many years faithful and devoted ladies have laboured there for the moral and spiritual elevation of their swarthy sisters. Till within the last few years months might pass and not a stranger visit the lonely missionary outpost, and still it shed its light, and made a little bit of Africa brighter and purer. Its agents toiled on, and the promise shone out from heaven as of old, and made them glad.

On Tuesday I left Qumbu for Gatberg, accompanied by Mr. Brownlee, who was ordered there to take temporary charge of the Residency, our old friend Mr. Thompson having died a few days previously. During the day we travelled through a large section of the Qumbu district, having taken a somewhat circuitous route. Large portions of it, scores of miles in extent, were then unoccupied, but it is beyond question one of the finest tracts of country in all South Africa for native occupation, and hence for missionary operations.

In the afternoon we arrived at the spot where Umhlonhlo consummated his treachery and murdered his Magistrate, Mr. Hamilton Hope. We turned aside to visit his lonely grave, which, marked by a rude cairn and roughly sculptured stone, is situated in a wildly romantic spot, a spot closely resembling many scenes in his native Scotland. As we stood by the grave with heads uncovered, our thoughts wandered involuntarily to events of recent occurrence and the providential escapes of many of our friends and acquaintances, notably my companion's father; while our conversation naturally took a somewhat sober if not sad turn. Poor Hope! he died in the discharge, only too faithfully, of what he regarded as his duty, and left life's scene, to him somewhat chequered and eventful, in the prime of life. May he be the last, as he has been the first, Magistrate murdered in cold blood by the chief and people whose interests he is appointed to watch over and guard.

But the shades of evening are fast approaching, and our camping ground is still far distant, so we dispel gloomy thoughts by a rapid ride, continued till after darkness had surrounded the scene. Arrived at a ruined village we select an old cattle fold as the warmest spot in which to spend the night, and soon have a blazing fire with "spits" in full working order. Our coffee, in the first instance, was a failure, but on being vigorously stirred with a *blazing fire stick* the sediment subsided and its flavour greatly improved. After partaking of a hearty supper we made our beds under the starry vault. The moon was at the full, and the dark forests on the opposite side of the narrow ravine where we encamped had a peculiarly weird appearance, while the hoot of the owl and the cry of various birds and animals gave to the whole surrounding a feeling of solitude and desolation. And the stars, they blinked so cold, one felt as if each were not "a diamond in the sky," but an ice point "reflecting frozen light," which penetrated through our warmest rugs to our very bones. When the clatter of tongues by the camp fire ceased, sleep stole upon me, and dreaming of truancy from school and blaeberries on the sunny slopes of Morven, I fell asleep, nor did I awake till the eastern sky proclaimed the coming day. A hasty toilet by a mountain brook, and a light breakfast dispatched, we were again in the saddle, and for hour after hour, till 8 P.M., when we arrived at Gatberg, we toiled through wild narrow gorges, over mountain passes all but impracticable, and through rough broken ground which sorely tried the temper and endurance of our horses.

It was not without a feeling of sadness I approached Gatberg. Mr. Thompson, to whom I had written of my intended visit, was in his grave, and instead of the cheery welcome I expected, and would have received, I, on the following day, visited the mound of earth which covers his mortal part in the tiny cemetery close by his garden wall.

On my arrival becoming known, the people came to meet me, and gave me an equally cordial welcome as was accorded me at Qumbu the previous week.

The services on the following Sunday were in all respects similar to what took place at Qumbu the previous Sabbath. The audience numbered over ninety; twenty-three persons partook of the Eucharist, while thirteen, including adults and infants, were admitted into the Church by baptism. I dispensed the Sacrament of the Lord's Supper to forty-nine persons and baptised eighteen during my journey.

In such a journey, however, there is much done which cannot be recorded in any written statement. Advice is given to one; admonition to another; a hint how to act in given circumstances to a third; school matters are arranged with head-men, and the work generally, in those distant and somewhat desolate regions, put into such shape that it will go on till the next visit is paid to the district, and a fresh impulse given to our somewhat feeble agencies there.

Here I must pause to describe briefly the place where Divine service was held at Gatberg. The "church," as they term it, is a cave, a regular rock cavern, as is seen along by St. Abb's Head and elsewhere on the British coast. In the persecuting days in Scotland it would have been invaluable. Presbyterian service has been held in many strange places, including floating churches where land was refused; but rarely with such peaceful surroundings have the sacraments been dispensed in a like situation. And yet there was no feeling of incongruity any more than there is at the great open-air gatherings in the Highlands of Scotland; and, indeed, as the singing of the congregation reverberated from rock to rock it strongly recalled scenes, all but forgotten, by the silent sea-shore in the land of my birth.

There was, I say, no sense of incongruity. The people are poor, the country is wild and mountainous; and what more natural than that they should take advantage of the shelter Nature provides to worship God there? Indeed, if any ecclesiastical building is consecrated, this must needs be. Is it not God's own workmanship, let us explain its formation on what scientific theory we will?

This "church," then, has an extreme length of thirty-four feet, by an average width of ten feet, and about nine to twelve feet high. It has been smoothly and firmly floored with clay and fitted with rough benches round its sides, while at the extreme interior an old sea-chest, whence procured I know not, set on end, serves as a pulpit. Leading up to the entrance amidst huge boulders and detached rocks, rude steps have been constructed, while access to the body of the "church" is through the fork of a tree growing V shaped, and completely concealing the entrance. Abundance of light streams in through a great cleft in the rock, but it is so situated that no rain enters.

On the day after dispensing the sacraments at Gatberg I started for home, and after three days of toilsome travel reached the Idutywa, sadly in need of "putting into some port to repair damage and refit," having in my journey gone over three hundred and fifty miles of very indifferent roads, and having been brought safely to its end by merciful Providence.

Both districts were at that time largely unoccupied, but were being rapidly filled, both by returning rebels and by people from the Colony, our own stations included. Both districts were placed under the same special laws, having been concerned in the rebellion, and the new arrangements made are much more satisfactory, and give greater security to life and property, than anything that had hitherto existed in those regions.

After making a minute inspection of the various sites proposed for new stations, and the prospects of people being settled near them, I returned to Duff. I had travelled three hundred and fifty miles, much of it through uninhabited country, and met with no serious accident to man or beast. The recommendations of the report I laid before the Mission Committee in Scotland were ultimately adopted, and in 1885 I was directed to proceed to that district to finally organise the Mission into regular stations. Three centres, unoccupied by European missionaries, were ultimately formed.

Of the Duff Mission and its work much need not be said. After I recovered from my accident I went over the whole district, and had interviews with all the head-men. The following conversation, which I transfer from my journal, is characteristic of the reception one meets with from most Africans at the first :—

15*th November.*—Visited Ludonga, and had a long interview with himself and his principal councillors; was not able to make any very satisfactory arrangement about certain candidates for baptism. He said he had no objection to my coming there to " speak " to his people and to read the Book, but that any of them going " after us " was another matter; he could not allow that. Being asked why he should object if they remained orderly and loyal subjects, he said that there were many reasons—very many. When still further pressed, he told me plainly that the "customs" were against it, and I was trying to bring in new things, and waxing eloquent, continued: "These girls will want money to buy dress; they will next learn to read; then they will despise our ignorance, and refuse to work for us; they will not grind corn nor make beer. When we want them to marry, they will say they must not marry one they do not love, and all our ways will be changed by them. Yes, I have heard of this before. It is always the same. The missionary comes to our people first, and he says he is going to teach us. We give him a place to build his house and a garden. He builds a school; and one day we see another man with a waggon and goods, and he builds a store. Things go on like this till there is a quarrel. The *Johnies*— soldiers—bring a cannon, and after that the chief of the soldiers comes and says, 'We have conquered this country, and it belongs to the Queen.' All you white people understand one another. You are too cunning for the black man. The black people wanted to be honest, but you were not. No, my daughters are not going to go after you. I have spoken."

Sunday, 3rd December.—A messenger arrived to say that two of our church members had been killed by lightning the previous afternoon, and wishing me specially to attend the funeral that day. I went. A large crowd of heathens gathered on a rising ground about five hundred yards distant. None of them would come near the house or burying place. Touching a body killed by lightning, or any one who has been in contact with such, is fraught with danger. After the funeral I approached the crowd, intending to preach. They fled like a flock of sheep attacked by wolves. I could not get within speaking distance of one of them, nor would they come near any of our native Christians who had been at the funeral.

27th December.—Visited Sigidi, and arrived just as a beer drinking, attended by about one hundred and fifty men, besides women and boys, began. I was *not* made welcome, but I was determined to ignore every hint, and remain to hold a religious service as a preliminary! Something like the following dialogue took place :—" Sigidi, I have come to preach to your people." " Yes, I am glad to see the missionary, but my friend is very ill." " I shall go to see him, perhaps I may cure him." " He is not here; he is far away." " Then we shall have service first." " These people came on business." " Then talk the business and I shall wait." . " It will keep the missionary long; better for him to come another time." " No, this is the best time; we shall begin now." Poor Sigidi sat through a half-hour's service with the look of a martyr; but when he found it was so brief he cheered up, complimented me on the sermon I had preached, and said, " It was good, very good to-day."

Speaking of native appreciation of sermons reminds me of a compliment once paid to me, and which had the virtue of sincerity. I was illustrating something,

I do not in the least recollect what, but as I brought the illustration to a point an old councillor, who probably had heard very few sermons, saw the aptness of the figure, and in the middle of the discourse exclaimed, "True; that is right," as he would have done in one of their own law courts if a pleader made a good point.

The year 1883 was the busiest I spent in Africa. As I read over the pages of my journal I wonder how I managed to wriggle through. Within the year I travelled 3400 miles on horseback, and spent one hundred and fifteen nights away from home. Some of these in mission-houses, some in hotels, a few in any shanty where I could find shelter, and many camping under canvas, or without any shelter beyond a clump of bushes. It was during this and the following year that, by quarterly visits, the foundation was laid for the Missions in East Griqualand.

On the 1st of January I left with Mr. Young to fix upon a site for the new mission-station of Main. After a search of ten or twelve days, during which we suffered much discomfort through having to camp out in wet and cold weather, we succeeded in our object, and after completing the necessary negotiations, we proceeded on our homeward journey. We parted a few miles from the Mbulu Mission, Mr. Young proceeding to Blythswood, I to Mbulu.

On the afternoon of the 14th, I left Mbulu with my wife, who was there on a visit, to return home. When we reached the Tsomo, it was flooded and we could not ride across. We were reluctant to return, and resolved to swim. We were accompanied by Mr. Davidson's son, who was to spend some days with us. He and I—we could only get one native swimmer to help—crossed and recrossed the river swimming five times, carrying clothes, saddles, &c., my wife also had to swim across with our assistance. After dressing, we caught and saddled our horses as if nothing unusual had happened. Swimming and at the same time carrying bundles above water, I found very exhausting work, and was not sorry when I saw the last taken across. The next day, we reached home to rest a week, and then start on a similar and much more protracted and arduous journey to East Griqualand.

After protracted negotiations, the site of the present Somerville—called after the late Dr. Somerville of Glasgow—was fixed, and a grant of 4000 acres of woodland and plain given to the Mission. Of all our stations in Africa, Somerville is the most picturesquely situated, and that which has most convenience of pasture, wood, and water. The scene from the manse windows is one that could hardly be surpassed. Situated on a slightly rising ground, there is an undulating plain of about a mile straight in front, and beyond that, trending away to the left, a range of mountains showing every variety of form and colour. Forests cover every hollow, and the brilliant blossom of trees and rich carpeting of flowers cannot be described in words. To the right, Tsolo rises from the plain like a solitary pyramid by ancient Nile, and, away beyond it, one can see undulations of hill and dale for a distance of forty miles. The scene to the west is equally grand, but the mountains being far distant, it has not the exquisite beauty of wood and falling water with moss-grown rock that the hills immediately in front of the Mission possess.

On turning over the pages of my journal during this period, I find but little variety in the work. Long journeys and reports of interviews with headmen and chiefs. Brief notes about school affairs and anniversary meetings. Building operations at Cunningham and Duff. Dispensing of ordinances at the various centres. Examining and admitting candidates by baptism. These and such duties filled up the days and months, leaving no time for recreation or study. It was nothing but work — work early and work late. Every other duty had to stand aside and wait till the inevitable happened, and I found that I must stop. But one's personal ailments are of no public interest, and I shall not inflict physician's prescriptions upon my indulgent readers.

Early in 1884, my wife, who had suffered from repeated attacks of fever, had to pay a visit to this country, and did not return till the end of the following year. By that time, I had removed to Somerville, and the new mission-house was nearly finished before her arrival.

Our Mission was not the only one that made rapid strides during the years immediately after the war.

Our United Presbyterian brethren extended their work in all directions. At Emgwali, they opened a new school for girls at a cost of over £3000. The station of Malan was built, and a beginning made with their Bomvanaland Mission. The Mbulu Mission, which under Mr. Davidson is the most perfectly organised and successful of all the Presbyterian Missions, was extended in various directions. Nor was the movement confined to Presbyterianism. The Church of England and Wesleyans put forth noble efforts to reconstruct what had been destroyed during the war, and to plant new stations in fields hitherto unoccupied. It was during this time of movement and re-adjustment of agencies that most of my travelling through hill and dale was done. I made many careful observations of the habits of certain animals, and gathered specimens which were afterwards arranged and placed in boxes. These were put away till such time as I might have an opportunity of submitting them to scientific authorities in Europe. I closed and sealed the boxes with the greatest care, but the white ants, disregarding locks and patent screws, made an entrance for themselves, and passing upwards from box to box left me only a few crystals which must have disagreed with their digestive organs. This; or they regarded crystals as seamen do "junk," an article that kept well, and could be used after the fresh meat of spider, bug, and beetle was exhausted.

I was once left in a curious fix by a roguish

servant. I had arranged to drive from Cunningham to King William's Town with Mr. Ross, and sent a young man in my employ with a bag containing a change of clothing to meet me there. He had plenty of time, and his load was light. Instead of going directly to his destination, he first visited some friends where a beer-drinking was being held. In order to appear respectable, as, sure, a " minister's man" ought to be, he exchanged his own corduroys for my broadcloth, and appeared among his friends as a "real gentleman." There he remained two whole days the admired and courted of all. At Cunningham, I found neither man nor bag, and had to proceed and subsequently appear on the platform at a public function in very old "riding togs." I was excessively angry, that of course, but, at the same time, felt some anxiety about the safety of my messenger. On my return the mystery was solved, for my "best coat" stank of stale beer and red ochre. Before my arrival, the wily savage had made a moonlight flitting, nor could the hounds of the law ever find a trace of him.

The toil and monotony of life during those busy years was now and then enlivened by pleasant as well as by comical incidents. The late Dr. Somerville visited the Transkei in 1883. His very presence was a source of renewed strength. Even our dull-witted Kaffirs named him "The old man who is young," and were greatly taken with his manner and pointed remarks. Of his public addresses I need say nothing, the whole English-speaking world knows their character and power, and many men of other nations, who only heard them through an interpreter, felt something of their fervour and fire; but I may be permitted to place on record the impression made on my own mind, and on the minds of others in Africa, by his private conversation.

After the day's work was done, and the doctor, refreshed by a cup of very sweet tea, found himself surrounded by a group of young people, it was easy to get him to talk. He delighted in giving others the benefit of his wide experience as a traveller and preacher. Speaking for myself I got from him in one evening a more distinct impression of the conditions of life in Australia and New Zealand than all my reading gave me. His pictures were drawn from life, and were presented to the mind in living form. Then he was full of old world lore and legend. His life-size drawings of Chalmers, Moncreiff, Thomson, and other heroes of the Non-Intrusion party, were only equalled by his clever cartoons of English statesmen poring over the institutions of the Scottish Church about the years 1838 to 1842.

From such themes he would suddenly change, as by a natural transition, to something bearing on each human life. By a few bold touches he brought common facts into such strong relief as to impress them indelibly upon the memory. Nor was he free from an impatience of manner if anything irritated him, but this rather helped to give piquancy to one's intercourse with him. I remember one evening when his conversation was more interesting than usual, and I, very tired after a hard day's work, but kept from falling asleep by my anxiety to hear what he said, unfortunately yawned. The doctor suddenly stopped and in a few moments retired to his room. We could not at the time understand why he had so abruptly closed a most interesting conversation. The mystery was explained the following morning on my wife asking him a question about the subject on which he had been speaking the previous evening. The reply was characteristic. He said, " I was going to tell you that last night, but I noticed your husband yawn, and I never continue a conversation if any one yawns."

The Rev. Charles Gordon of Douglas circumnavigated Africa in 1884, and spent some months in Kaffraria. His visits were very greatly prized. He was in full sympathy with men beginning life, and being conversant with the movements of modern thought, conversation with him had a very special charm for many of us.

While in Africa he collected an armoury of weapons of war that could serve for a campaign, and musical instruments of wonderful form and still more wonderful notes sufficient to furnish an orchestra. I parted from him in the Transkei with deepest regret that his visit had been so short. He proceeded to the coast and thence to Eastern Africa, to carry the dregs of its deadly fever to Scotland. I returned to my work and six months camping under canvas in laying the foundations of the East Griqualand Missions. To him the natives applied the sobriquet of "The beautiful fat minister."

While "The beautiful fat minister" was in the Transkei, he one day found himself engaged in very confidential conversation with a wily old chief. This man, though well acquainted with Europeans, professed to know nothing of the white man or his ways, and Mr. Gordon, always the soul of courtesy, answered his questions, and entered into explanations of many points on which the chief professed himself ignorant. They discussed politics, war, religion, social customs, land tenure, the division of labour, and the proper sphere of woman; her price on becoming a wife was a point on which they could not agree. The African maintained that her insubordination would be unendurable unless the purchase cattle were in her father's kraal, and could be reclaimed the moment she showed any signs of disobedience. She would neither brew beer nor attend on her husband's friends if she once felt her independence, or dreamt that she was on an equality with her lord. The Scotchman argued that as long as woman was regarded as a chattel, and kept a drudge and domestic slave, that the Africans could never become a great nation; that to the emancipation of woman was due, in great measure, the prosperity and power of Great Britain, and that similar results would follow a more enlightened social policy in Africa.

When agreement between them was found to be

impossible the chief took a pinch of snuff, rose, shook himself, and, as if preparing to take his departure, said to his companion, "How many wives have you got yourself?" This was a staggering question coming from an African to a bachelor after a discussion on the purchase price of woman, but there was nothing for it but to tell the truth, and he replied, "I have no wife." The old man assumed that look of pity and commiseration which only Africans can assume, and in accents tremulous with feigned sympathy said, "Is that because you could not get the cattle?" Before his victim could reply, the son of the desert was off without uttering another word.

VIII.

EAST GRIQUALAND—NEW MISSIONS—NOVEL EXPERIENCES.

ON the 21st of July, 1885, in obedience to instructions received from Scotland to proceed to East Griqualand "to organise the Mission and build the manse," I left Duff on horseback. A small travelling waggon with what necessaries I required had preceded me, but, according to an unvarying African rule, arrived some days after it was due, to our no small inconvenience. My stock of necessaries was not large. It consisted of a bell tent, blankets, rugs, bedding, tinned meats, coffee, tea, and sugar. I also carried a quantity of salt, as a convenient medium of exchange. In regions where the soil is devoid of saline properties native children often prefer a pinch of salt to the most tempting sweets, while domestic animals cannot be kept away from a spot where either salt or brine has been spilled.

My camp-followers were my groom, cook, evangelist, a boy to herd horses and cattle, and the inevitable "handy man." For the accommodation of

European tradesmen who were to follow a second tent had to be provided. A temporary shanty was erected for the native servants. The first few weeks after my arrival were spent in visiting head-men and others interested in our movements, and making as many friends as I possibly could, knowing that much depended on how we were at first received. I succeeded beyond my expectations, and was able, with assistance given by other members of the Mission, to fix upon a second centre, and complete the negotiations for what is now the Buchanan Mission.

By the middle of August building operations were fairly under way. The masons had got their trenches dug, and were busy getting in the foundations. The brickmaker had his crowd of naked savages merrily dancing in a mud-hole preparing clay for the moulds, while the woodman's axe resounded in the forest felling timber for brick burning, and to be sawn into planks and beams for the building. I was well satisfied with the progress made, and felt that, weather and other conditions being favourable, the work would be finished long before the time upon which we calculated.

The nights were very cold and snow fell at intervals, making life under canvas very uncomfortable. We were at an elevation of 3600 feet above the level of the sea, and the wind from the snow-clad Drakensberg Range was cruelly keen for weeks after our arrival. The previous summer had been one of extreme drought, and the failure of their crops had reduced many of the natives to the verge of starvation, and now the severe winter cut off their cattle in tens of thousands. Hide merchants made a fortune in a few months. Sheep were in equally evil plight with the horned cattle.

Fresh provisions, even fowls, were in the circumstances very difficult to procure, and when procured were poor emaciated things, fit neither to boil nor roast. This brought me that most trying experience, living on tinned meats. A sardine at lunch does very well when one knows that he can have the choice of something else for dinner, but when for weeks one's breakfast consists of coffee, bread, and tinned meat; his lunch of bread, tinned meat, and coffee; and his dinner of tinned meat, coffee, and bread, he feels like that Irishman who varied his diet by potatoes and point and point and potatoes. After a fortnight of it one has the feeling that a common flavour, or no flavour at all, pervades everything, and that it makes little difference whether the coffee is stirred into the meat or the sugar into the coffee, for fish, fowl, and flesh taste exactly alike. As Professor Drummond says, one would eat the tins themselves but for the sense of hardness.

As our work progressed I found myself face to face with an unexpected but serious difficulty. Our brick kilns were fully half-a-mile from the building, and owing to the extreme poverty of stock of all kinds, I found it impossible to procure waggons for the conveyance of bricks to the builders. For a day or two it seemed as if the work must come to a standstill, and the men be discharged at great inconvenience to them and to me, as well as at considerable loss to the Mission. In this difficulty it suddenly occurred to me that what I could not get done by ordinary beasts of burden, I might accomplish by the labour of women. After a brief mental calculation, I resolved to put my idea to the proof. I knew there was a good deal of want and suffering among the native people, and that food would be to many more welcome than any other form of payment; especially to the women who in times of scarcity suffer most. I sent a message to several villages to say that if twenty women came on the following day, I would give them a day's work at sixpence each, and a good meal. Nineteen came. I gave each a small square of board, and then told them they were to bring a certain tale of bricks, after which they would receive their day's wages. They had never done such work, and there was a good deal of hesitation among them, but at last they consented to try it for one day. By 2.30 P.M. they came to claim their wages, having honestly fulfilled their bargain, and highly pleased with their employment. The following day over forty applied. They carried the bricks on their heads supported on the boards. In this way we conveyed 100,000 bricks for the manse and church, at cheaper rates than by ordinary means of transport, and with hardly any loss from breakage. This system I recommend to others similarly situated.

We were now, as I thought, on a fair way to

finishing our work without further interruption, but another and a more formidable difficulty arose. It was small-pox. Twice within this century small-pox had ravaged South Africa, and was dreaded as men dread the plague. It now appeared in our immediate neighbourhood. The family where it broke out were, heathen fashion, driven from the homes and habitations of men to seek shelter with the beasts of the forest. While there they were not allowed to approach a human being or come near their old dwelling. The food and little comforts they left in their home they were not permitted to take away. No one supplied their wants. They were cut off from the living by a more terrible sentence than ever was pronounced on leper by a self-satisfied priest. It was no wonder that first one, then another and another died, and with harrowing details of suffering, details in the case of a mother who gave birth to a child when covered with eruption, so horrible that I dare not transfer them to these pages. At last there were left a little boy of nine, who was very ill, his aunt, who had been a member of his father's household, and a woman friend. The two women were not affected, and in order to save themselves resolved to go to a distant part of the country, and seek shelter and food from those who were in ignorance of their having been in contact with small-pox patients. The boy they tied to a tree with a bit of grass-rope, and left him either to perish of disease and hunger or to be devoured by wild beasts, with which the forest abounded.

The poor little fellow managed to undo the rope and crawled to my encampment. He arrived at dusk on a bitterly cold evening, perfectly naked, and suffering from a severe attack of confluent small-pox. How he expected help from me I do not know. He was the son of heathen parents, who had but little intercourse with Europeans. He may have, in his heathen home, heard something of the Christian and the Christian's God, for these things do travel, and are spoken of in places where we should hardly expect to find any trace of Christian influence. Be that as it may, come he did, and passed several native houses on his way. I went out to see him as he crouched in the rough, tangled grass, the picture of a wounded animal. Only once did I see such another sorry sight, and that was on the only occasion on which I ever pulled a trigger at a monkey. The creature fell, sorely wounded, and as I approached the spot it gazed at me with large lustrous eyes from behind a fallen tree with a look which seemed to say, "You might have done better," and attempted to staunch a wound with its paw. I turned away, sickened by the sight, and never shot another monkey. With such a wild, appealing look in his large black eyes did the creature before me watch my movements as I approached him. He was perfectly naked, and his little bones showed through his skin so as to give him more the appearance of a skeleton than a living being. I was in a fix. I had no shelter, not even a shed, where I could give him protection from the weather. The night was biting cold. It was plain that unless something was done for him he would perish before morning. I brought him a thick woollen blanket, and some warm food. He must have been nearly starved, for he devoured the bread and milk I had mixed for him like a famished dog. After hearing the remainder of his story, I directed him to the shelter of a small cave near the edge of the forest. Next day I visited him, bringing food and fuel soaked with paraffine. I kindled a large fire, and left him for another day.

No sooner did it become known that I had had communication with the "sickness people" than I was vigorously boycotted. Before this I spent an hour every morning vaccinating. After it none came for that or any other purpose. My labourers struck or deserted me. My personal attendants muttered rebellion. A deputation of Christian (?) people came to urge that if I continued " to feed the boy and keep alive the sickness, no one would come to service on Sundays." I felt provoked beyond endurance, and the reply to the deputation was laconic, if not satisfactory. It was this :—" I shall keep and care for the boy if they don't come to church till the day of judgment."

Yet another difficulty arose. My groom told me he heard a whisper as if there was an intention on the part of our heathen neighbours to kill my patient, and so " put the sickness under the earth." No other case had appeared in the district. I sent for the head-man, and after some persuasion induced him to come within easy-speaking distance, keeping well to windward of me. I told him that any one seen approaching the cave would be shot. Black-hearted fear would keep them away at night, if I could secure his safety during the day. Two days after this interview a hardy individual, wishing to test the value of my threat, approached the forbidden spot. A rifle bullet, sent whistling past him at a safe distance, made him fly in headlong hurry, leaving his kaross behind him. A second made him feel " that I died that day."

After this I nursed my patient through his illness without further molestation, and finally brought him to the Mission. No sooner was this done, and danger of infection past, than his relatives came to claim him and bring him home. This I resisted, and the matter came before the Courts of law. At the trial something like the following took place :—Magistrate to boy—" Do you wish to remain at the Mission or go home to your friends?" " I wish to be with those who took me when I was dead." The uncle was then asked what he had done for him, and replied that he did not require to do anything, " as the missionary had taken charge of the boy." Questioned as to the boy's father's property, he gave the number of sheep and cattle he had. Then came the verdict, to this effect : —" You are to have the care of your late brother's cattle in trust for your nephew. Their milk is to be your reward. You will be held responsible to this Court for the animals and their increase at any time you may be called upon to give an account of them. Your nephew is to remain at the Mission, and Mr. Macdonald is to be his guardian till he comes of age." The uncle's face after this judgment was a study. He not only lost the boy but was burdened with the care and responsibility of cattle which he had already quietly appropriated, and made accountable to the Court. I do not know whether the Magistrate administered sound law or not, but it is certain he administered sound sense.

After this, my boy attended school, and did odds and ends about the Mission, transferring much of his affection to my wife, who had now returned from Scotland. Before we left Africa, I had the satisfaction of placing him under the fatherly care of Dr. Stewart at Lovedale, where he remains. He is supported there by the Sabbath School of Free St. Andrew's Congregation, Edinburgh.

To establish the Mission on a permanent footing, it was necessary to become personally acquainted with all the men of importance in the district, and to this duty I now addressed myself. I made long journeys, generally extending to five or six days. These journeys had necessarily much in common, but I never went from home but I met with something of interest, either in the ways and habits of the people, or in brake, bush, or cairn. It was during these wanderings I made what observations I could of the habits of animals and the geological formation of the country. To a few of these reference will be made in a closing chapter.

K

Many of the head-men received me cordially, and readily gave facilities for settling evangelists among them. Others made excuses. There had been no harvest; they were hungry, and must wait "till the children are carrying bundles of sweet cane—sorgum, and the people are eating green maize and drinking plenty of beer and milk." It would be impossible to think of a teacher or listen to his words "while the children were crying with hunger in the huts." A few were openly hostile, and would on no terms permit Christians to settle among them. Curiously, some of these were, in a few months, among my staunchest friends and warmest supporters. In one location there was a Christian woman—the only Christian there, living with heathen relatives. She came to me frequently urging me to send an evangelist to them. The head-man refused permission on the ground that he could not give a garden without depriving others of their rights. I then appointed the woman herself the preacher, and so well did the arrangement answer, that there is now a flourishing out-station in that location, and the head-man is one of its most cordial supporters.

Another head-man refused point plank to discuss the question of an evangelist with me. Two months later I relieved a favourite of his from severe physical pain by a simple surgical operation. This broke down his opposition. After it, nothing was too good for me, and no kindness too great for the Mission I represented.

Near the sources of the Umtata, I met an old acquaintance, Hai-Hai, whose two daughters were accidentally shot by young Murray. He had emigrated there some years before, and having carried his Bible along with him, began to preach its doctrines. When I first visited his location, he had gathered round him quite a community of Christian believers, several of whom I baptised. It is because we find such men as Hai-Hai among the rank and file of African Christians that we continue to believe in Missions to the heathen and in the future of heathen peoples.

In a distant mountain valley, near the highest spurs of the Drakensberg Range, I found a small community of Christians who had emigrated from the Colony. They were a mixture of Basutos, Fingoes, and Hottentots. My first religious service among them was very peculiar. I spoke in English, which was interpreted into Kaffir, and then successively into Sesuto and Dutch—the latter for the Hottentots who knew no other language. On my return journey, I ascended a high mountain spur to examine the geological formation near the summit. I understood then, for the first time, how the Israelites could be supplied with such an abundance of quails. On the grassy ridges I met with them in countless numbers. They ran about the horses' feet in the grass; rose in shoals within a few yards of us, and hopped about like sparrows in a barn yard. They are migratory in their habits, and were making their way across the mountain chain.

I once, in the interests of science, toiled through the valley of the Umga, the deepest, longest, and narrowest gorge I have seen in Africa, or out of it. The length of its narrow part is almost twenty miles. Its sides rise to an elevation of about 2000 feet, and the rocky summits are in many places not over half-a-mile apart. I was anxious to examine its geology and also unearth a few Bushmen who then inhabited a cave about the middle of the gorge. My success in the first was partial, and in the second I failed quite. My friends the Bushmen were famous rain makers, and had gone to a function in a neighbouring valley. I noticed one peculiarity worth recording. The morning had been windy—not stormy by any means. In the gorge, after I entered it, it blew such a hurricane that I could hardly stand in exposed places, and climbing among rocks was impossible. The noise made by the wind as it swirled and eddied among the rocks and crannies, was the most peculiar I ever heard. It sounded as if ten thousand discordant instruments were being twanged by the hand of a giant. I thought a tornado had sprung up and was raging on the plains above, but, on making inquiry in the evening, I found there had been nothing beyond a strong breeze since morning. Only one conclusion was possible, Æolus must have emigrated and taken up his abode among the corries of the Umga.

I once on a Saturday evening arrived at a place where I was to hold service on the following day. My camp-followers lost their way and did not arrive till Sunday forenoon. I had to go supperless and make my bed under a bush, where I slept with neither bedding nor covering. In the morning I had a bathe in a clear bubbling stream with a smooth pebbly bottom, where small garnets and rubies tumbled about with flakes of mica and specimens of porphery, a sure indication of the nature of the rocks in the distant hills. Being without toilet requisites, I manufactured a very serviceable comb from a slip of bark, it was not elegant, but appearances count for little in Africa. I have used a slab of stone as a plate, and a bit of shaped cowhide for a wine-cup. I have seen porridge stirred with an ox yoke-skey, and served in a straw hat. My horse's mane has done duty as a towel, and my saddle as a pillow, often. I have made my bed of hempen sacks, and slept soundly.

After spending a few months engaged in varied duties, I felt that, to carry out the plans formed, I must have assistance. From our own Mission I could get none. We had no one who could be sent, but our United Presbyterian brethren gave one of their number, the Rev. Mr. Stirling. After his arrival we rapidly extended the sphere of our operations, and ultimately the Mission was divided into two, when the Buchanan station was formed under Mr. Stirling as missionary. Over three hundred church members, and a number of baptised adherents, hived off from Somerville to Buchanan. So rapidly did the work grow that the twenty-five members who professed to belong to us in November, 1881, when the Rev.

Richard Ross last visited the district, had grown to over six hundred in March, 1887. In 1881 Mr. Ross wrote:—

"Gatberg was laid waste by the Pondomisi and Basutos; none of our people went off with the rebels. Some of them were killed fighting for the Queen. The two Church school-houses were burned; hence, at present the services are held in a large cave thirty-five by nine feet. Only twenty-five of the forty-six church members that were there before have returned to their burnt-down houses. I was there dispensing the sacrament of the Lord's Supper on 20th November."

The solitary station in the lonely Gatberg, with its cave church, a church for which I cherish very fond recollections, had become two well-equipped Missions, with thirty-two preaching stations, at which services were regularly held. The Mission had won the good-will of almost all the head-men, and its agents were made welcome wherever they went.

It is not to be supposed, however, that heathenism was either dead or moribund. Six hundred is a large number no doubt, when taken by itself, but when compared with the sixty thousand and more inhabitants of the district it becomes insignificant enough. The tinkling of the Sabbath bell was heard in many places, but in a far larger number the great bull-hide drum of heathen revelry resounded over mountain and plain. European dress had gained for itself toleration and respectability, but war-paint, charms, red ochre, feathers and magicians' fantasies, still held their own with undiminished publicity. In the immediate vicinity of the Mission, Sunday was observed as a day of rest, but in every forest the sound of the woodman's axe was heard, and teams of oxen laboured over the length and breadth of the land. Sufferers sought relief at the Mission or from physicians, but the witch doctor plied his craft, and applied his burning firestick to the sole of the victim's foot, to extort a confession, and thus create work for the surgeon or missionary, in restoring shrivalled tendons and charred muscles.

It is necessary to make these remarks, as there are many persons who think that the conversion of a few hundreds to Christianity should reform a whole province. It is not so. It never was so since the first dawn of the Kingdom of God. The growth of ideas has always been slow, and only by comparing one age with another can progress and improvement be marked. And this can be seen nowhere to better advantage than in South Africa. The newly-arrived European, set down at Lovedale, sees around him what he takes to represent savage life. Everything is new to him, and he daily feels the vast gulf that separates Western civilisation from African barbarism. If he proceeds inland the darkness deepens. Signs of intelligence, hardly noticed among the red blanket men of the Thumie, are now wanting. The knobkerrie gives place to the iron-headed spear. The woollen blanket to the sheep or antelope skin. The plough to the mattock, and the harrow to a forest bush. The ox, as a beast of burden, to the wife or daughter. The waggon is represented by a rough sledge, and the functions of the sickle are usurped by a short-handled assegai. Instead of an implement of English or American manufacture, the ancestral battle-axe does duty in the forest; while the saw and the plane are unknown and unrepresented.

If under these circumstances one meets with a native man or woman from the Colony, or who has been trained at such a place as Lovedale, it is apparent that a great step has been made towards a higher and better life. True it is that certain faculties seem to be lost. An old head-man, becoming impatient of the return of a young school teacher sent in search of strayed horses, said to the writer, " I must go myself to look for them. Whatever you may teach these young men to see in books, when they come back to us they can see nothing of what is around them." He spoke the truth. That extraordinary faculty of following on the trail of animals, and which is incredible to those who have not witnessed it, can only be acquired by constant practice from childhood. A boy at five or six begins life herding calves. Every day he watches their movements; follows their tracks; notices how they nibble grass, lie down, or drink water. After a few years he is promoted to the care of sheep, goats, or cattle, and continues the same habit of constant observation. By the time he reaches manhood, certain of his faculties are abnormally developed, while his intelligence lies dormant. The boy, on the other hand, who attends school has his intellectual faculties awakened, while those others which are chiefly of use in the old savage life, receive no further development than in the case of Europeans.

I have once and again met with traces of this civilising influence in distant parts. Young women married to heathen husbands carry the use of the needle into the new and often uncongenial home. Widows left with the care of children support themselves by doing laundry work for soldiers at distant outposts. Young carpenters and smiths carry the mysteries of their respective crafts with them, and from shapeless log or rusty bar produce articles which are the wonder of a whole village.

But is not the African incorrigibly lazy? Such is the question asked, and very naturally, by the reader of modern books of travel and popular fiction. No, he is not. There is nothing lazy about him. He is in precisely the same position as the "masher" whose time is spent between his club, popular promenades, and the theatre. Neither have any work to do. Each enjoys himself after his kind, and that is the end of it. Africans when they have any motive for work can and do exert themselves. In war and hunting they undergo severe and long-continued fatigue. At the diamond fields tens of thousands of them work from year to year at labour of a most trying nature. The same may be said of every shipping port in the Colony. There never is any difficulty in procuring gangs of men when fair remuneration is offered, and when well fed their labour compares favourably with ordinary unskilled European labour.

At their own homes the men do not work. They care for the cattle and milk them. They also perform certain duties at seed and harvest time, but during the greater part of the year all manual labour is left to the women. The men are the "mashers." Beer drinking represents the club; court trials the theatre, and public dances the popular promenades of European watering-places. At such gatherings the African dandy can show to advantage the pattern of his blanket, the splendour of his armlets and rings, as well as the elegance of his much tormented hair.

Even into this aimless idle life some hazy notion of Christianity finds it way now and then long before the advent of the missionary, and this is very well illustrated in the circumstance I am about to relate. A heathen chief, Jojo, living at a distance of nearly one hundred miles from Somerville, repeatedly sent messages to say he wished to see me, and asking me to pay a visit to his country. I at first sent evasive answers, thinking the old man simply wished to gratify his curiosity by having me as his guest. He at last became so persistent and pressing that I consented to go, and late in February, 1886, I left for his country accompanied by the Rev. Mr. Stirling and the usual camp following. Heavy rains had fallen the previous week, and our first experience was having to strip before crossing the river below the mission-house. The day was hot and the water warm, but one

must get used to Africa before he can with perfect
equanimity cross a swollen river *a la* Kaffir. We
had similar experiences at the Tsitsa, Tina, and
Umsimvubu. The Umsimthlava we found foaming
down with such volume and rapidity that we deemed
it prudent not to attempt its passage for a day, and
spent a very uncomfortable night on its southern
bank. The following day we crossed in safety, and
in another hour found ourselves, on Thursday forenoon, in Jojo's kingdom. We dispatched a messenger
to acquaint the great man of our arrival. He sent his
son to bid us welcome and appoint a day for a formal
reception. This was the following Monday. At the
appointed hour Jojo appeared round the corner of a
green sloping hill, followed by two thousand mounted
warriors. This would be the proper courtesy to a
representative of Government; to two travel-stained
missionaries it was an exceptional honour. We soon
discovered that the old man was in earnest in asking
me to visit him. He did wish to have a missionary
in his country. There were no Christians there, and
there had never been any, but he had heard good
reports of Somerville from his most trusted councillor,
who had been sent to make inquiries about myself
and my doings. He could now see no good reason
why I should not remain with him there and then.
If I did not remain, why should not Mr. Stirling?
They would build a house and give a good garden.
What more could heart of man desire?

After a long conference we were invited to select a

site for a Mission whenever we chose, and guides supplied for that purpose. We spent a day searching for a suitable spot, and were rewarded by having about 1200 acres of their best land set apart for our use at any time we choose to take possession. It is satisfactory to be able to add, that the United Presbyterian Church sent a missionary to Jojo, and that he is now engaged in his important work at a Mission begun under the somewhat peculiar circumstances just described.

On our return journey we separated to visit various places where we had agents at work. When I arrived at Somerville I found the river at the Mission in flood. After a little hesitation I decided to swim across. I tied my clothes on the pommel of the saddle, and drove the horses into the river. They crossed easily. My groom followed next, and I brought up the rear. The current was strong, but there was no particular danger in crossing. Our troubles were not yet ended, for the horses thought they had done enough work, and, instead of allowing themselves to be caught, galloped home carrying our garments along with them. The black man, accustomed to go barefooted, ran after them nimbly enough, I followed, limping through the tangled grass as best I could. Such are some of the experiences of life in the African Mission.

Missionaries have been accused, and that on high authority, of living in luxury, and that condition of ease and indolence implied by luxurious living. My experience among them has been otherwise. Speaking for myself I can confidently say that, during the last five years I spent in Africa, my missionary income would barely suffice to keep me in road money doing my proper work. This left no margin for the luxurious living of which we have heard so much; and as to indolence and ease, I found none. When a man travels, in twelve months, a distance exceeding 3000 miles on horseback, it is enough to show that he does not live in idleness. So far as my experience goes my case is by no means exceptional. Not many missionaries travel so much as I did, and for a very good reason. They could not do it and live on their incomes.

But does not Mr. Spurgeon and others, who are authorities, maintain that missionaries could be sent out at ninety pounds a-year each, to do the work now done by ordained men receiving four times that amount. I do not know. I can only say that I have not met any such. I paid my tradesmen in the Mission £120 per annum, and could not get them at a lower scale of wage. Their board and lodgings cost them thirty shillings per week, and their clothes forty per cent. higher than in England.

To this our detractors may reply, that men of self-denial might live on less than is paid at present to artisans. Precisely. We should then have a body of men engaged in raising heathens from barbarism to civilisation, and compelled to live under such conditions, that their own families must go to swell the ranks of barbarism or semi-barbarism. Nor is this all. I could have lived on our detractor's ninety pounds. I could have lived on less. By adopting native garb and living as natives do, it is marvellous what one can accomplish on ten pounds a-year, but had I lived these last five years on ninety pounds per annum I should have in all received no less a sum than four hundred and fifty pounds sterling, and I should have accomplished just that amount of work that any one of my numerous evangelists did, and their income was then ten pounds a-year. With ninety pounds I could not have kept a horse, whereas I kept four and had more than enough of work for them. I should thus be compelled to work at one spot, and the impression made would not be the one hundredth of what was actually done. I need not pursue this subject further; the project needs only to be stated to see its folly. Besides, I notice that those of our critics who have sons in the ministry, do not often send them to the Mission at ninety or at any other number of pounds annually. Is this in order to keep the young men from a life of luxury and effeminacy?

The inadequate conception the foregoing account of my own work gives of ordinary everyday life at a Mission station, makes no apology necessary for introducing a few pages descriptive of what goes on at the majority of the African Missions. Instead of stating, in general terms, the nature of the work, it will be better if I select some particular centre and explain in a few sentences what goes on there. Let us take the Mbulu, an average Mission centre, under admirable management. It was founded about twenty-five years ago by the Rev. Mr. Sclater, now of Manchester. From his principal centre he made short journeys in his waggon, which served both as a means of conveyance and as a dwelling in his travels. These journeys, extending to ten, fifteen or twenty miles, usually occupied eight to ten days. Halts were made at the larger villages and services held. A centre was also chosen in connection with each circuit, and then the missionary remained stationary for several days or even weeks. These centres gradually grew into out-stations, and the missionary's visits came to be looked forward to as regular events. In this way he made the acquaintance of a large number of people, and the prejudice against himself and the message he bore was gradually overcome. A school was opened and taught by a native Christian. Classes were conducted during the week for adult inquirers by the missionary, and audiences were given to all and sundry who came to him, no matter what their object.

To raise people from a state of barbarism to civilisation something more than precept is needed, and every wise missionary endeavours to make his station a model of industry and progress. Fencing, planting, irrigating, sowing and ornamenting are all as essential, in their proper place, as are the other duties connected with missionary life, and from the first the

Mbulu took its full share of such work, but it is under its present missionary, the Rev. James Davidson, that most has been done to develop its natural resources. A water race has been dug out. It irrigates a fine orchard, and is used by many native families to water their maize patches. No sooner was it finished than the missionary began to instruct the natives how to grow wheat, potatoes, and other garden produce, and now every square yard of ground under the level of the furrow is taken advantage of for these purposes. The Mission is not only a beacon of light: it is a home of industry also. The foundation laid was solid, and the structure is permanent. At the spots where Mr. Sclater, sitting in his waggon, used to speak to perhaps a dozen half-naked figures, there are now good substantial churches and prosperous schools. Men whose whole time was divided between beer-drinking and hearing causes, have discarded the savage life, and may be seen standing at the plate on Sunday morning as the church bell calls the worshippers together, and women whose only prospect was a dreary life of domestic slavery and thankless toil, have come to realise that there are higher objects to which they can attain than brewing beer and attending on their half-drunken husbands and their friends. These results are not produced without toil and anxiety. They cannot be given a healthy direction for the future of that people without intelligence and a clear understanding of the history and growth of nations. And this, I venture to say, can only be done by men of culture and learning, whether lay or clerical. Which it is to be will depend on many considerations of policy, both Mission and State. In any case, the uneducated man, however pious, will not find his sphere there.

* * * * * *

After the building operations at Somerville were completed, the church was opened in the usual Kaffir fashion. Twelve fat oxen, and twice that number of sheep and goats, were sacrificed on the altar of custom. The few Europeans in the district who were able to attend the meeting contributed £30 to the funds. Men of all denominations joined hands in seeking to promote the moral and spiritual welfare of a people but recently broken and scattered by war, and now slowly recovering from their losses, and gradually developing into a higher and better life.

My work was now finished, and we began to prepare for taking a final leave of Somerville. The missionary who was to take permanent charge of the station had arrived in the country, and had, during a brief visit to us, seen a good deal of the district. He had also got his first baptism of fire. One night, while he was at Somerville, a thunderstorm of more than ordinary severity passed over the station. It split a large tree close at hand into fragments, and did other damage about the premises. While it was at its height, my wife and I went to the window to admire the brilliant play of many-coloured lightning.

Not so our young friend, who evidently thought such conduct was a direct tempting of Providence. Before the time of writing these lines it is safe to say he has changed his mind about thunderstorms, and perhaps other storms also.

Before we left, our native friends collected a few pounds among themselves, to present to us as an acknowledgment of indebtedness to the Free Church of Scotland. The meeting at which it was presented was very touching. Maneli, my faithful evangelist, advanced, full of mystery, to make a speech. In his hand he held a small paper parcel, which, just as he began to speak, burst, sending a shower of silver coins all over the floor. The murder was out, and he, in a sentence, finished his statement. With the money we bought two lamps, which we prize far above their intrinsic worth. They remind us of some of our happiest days, days spent under conditions of outward discomfort, but with the satisfaction of being engaged in laying the foundation of a better and brighter era in East Griqualand.

There was nothing to detain us longer, and with many pleasant recollections of friendships made and new ties formed, we said adieu to our friends and turned our steps towards Europe. The first few miles we were accompanied by a large crowd on horseback to see us on our way. The women who had gathered at the station, one of whom brought an enormous pumpkin to give us as food for the journey, set up a wail of lamentation as we drove off in the " spider."

The men followed us several miles, and after another halt parted from us with a good hearty cheer.

We plodded on our way, through rain and swollen rivers, to the coast, and arrived in England to read the famous *fac-simile* letter in next morning's *Times*.

IX.

THE NATIVE AFRICANS—THEIR CUSTOMS AND HABITS.

IT is only within a very recent period that ethnology has become a scientific study, and the African Continent is to this day almost unbroken ground. The older missionaries paid but little attention to the habits and customs of the people among whom they laboured, except in so far as they bore some relation to their own work of bringing men under the influence of the Gospel. Heathen customs were regarded as revolting and immoral. They were not spoken of nor written about when it was at all possible to avoid them. I am not acquainted with any book which deals exhaustively with native customs and habits. Folk-lore and poetry is still practically unbroken ground. It is impossible to treat this subject exhaustively in a single chapter. It would require a volume to itself, and I intend to do no more than introduce my readers to the social primitive life and habits of the people before they came under the influence of European thought and civilisation. These are fast passing away in the southern portion of the continent, and much difficulty is at times experienced in distinguishing between what is ancient and properly African, and what is the result of European influence.

In any study of the customs of South African peoples, it is necessary to bear in mind that they are of very mixed origin, and that they have but a hazy notion regarding their original home. They all agree that they came from the north, but at what period it is impossible to determine. Nor can we trace to a common origin the various tribes, Hottentot, Bushmen, and Bantu, with whom Europeans have come into contact in the extreme south, while Damaras and Koranas cannot be classed with any of the tribes already enumerated.

Most of these tribes have, at one period or another, during the past two hundred years, been less or more in contact with Europeans. Shipwrecked sailors and even delicately reared ladies have lived and died among the tribes of the south-eastern seaboard, and contact with these must have influenced the primitive beliefs of a simple barbarous people. Again, since the first discovery of the Cape of Good Hope, daring spirits have not been wanting to engage in expeditions for hunting and discovery. These introduced to the native mind some hazy idea of fire-arms, and round this mystery has grown up a class of superstitions which it is very difficult to separate from what is ancient and belongs properly to native mythology.

In what follows every care has been taken to examine and compare doubtful customs and superstitions, and only that retained which seemed of undoubted antiquity, and which helped to throw light on the life and history of the people.

The tribes whose customs I am about to detail, Hottentots and Bushmen being excluded, are those occupying the south-eastern seaboard between the Cape Colony and Natal, and to a distance of about two hundred and fifty miles inland. Of these the best known are :—Gaikas, Gcalekas, Tembus, Pondos, Pondomisi, Xezibis, Hlubis, Basutos, and Fingoes, the last being a mixed people composed of fragments of many tribes. The Zulus also may be regarded as having in the main the same customs, law, and usages as those named. All the tribes, the Basutos excepted, speak a common language, with modifications of dialect, and pursue the same mode of life. They are tillers of the soil, and own herds and flocks. Their systems of law and government have much in common, and their religious beliefs are substantially the same. None of them have a written language, nor any means of making a permanent record of events. Dates are fixed by reference to some great public event, as war, famine, the appearance of a comet, or an eclipse. Laws are handed down by oral tradition, through a class of men whose whole time and attention is devoted to such work, while history is chiefly remembered in the form of song, commemorative of great victories, and deeds of valour done by men of renown.

The natives of South Africa are divided into tribes, clans, sub-clans, and families, much in the same manner as was customary among the ancient Celts. The hereditary rulers are regarded with the same veneration as were the Scottish chiefs of some centuries ago, and the head of a family not only rules his own household, but all his connections—sons, grandsons, younger brothers, and even cousins, if a man of standing and influence. Wealth is the usual passport to be regarded as the head of a family. Connection with some royal household is the only door to the most insignificant chieftainship. The origin of royalty is lost in the mists of antiquity, but in recent times men have, through military prowess, attained to the rank of chieftainship, but generally by means of successful revolt. They in turn, or their sons, usually pay the penalty of the usurper. The poison bowl tells no tales.

Though the respective tribes are divided from one another by sharp and well defined characteristics, we find that marriages between the families of paramount chiefs are common, and that almost all of them are connected by ties of blood. But such relationships do not preclude war ; they rather add to its rancour and horror when it does begin. Although the sons and daughters of paramount chiefs may marry, these worthies must never meet face to face themselves. If they did, one must salute the other, and salutation acknowledges superiority in rank of the chief saluted. If there is no salutation their followers fall to blows, and a struggle, leading to inter-tribal war, is the result. Subordinate chiefs have their order of precedence assigned them, and, when visiting in another tribe, always salute those whose guests they are, even when inferior in rank to themselves. I once invited two paramount chiefs to a public function. Each ascertained that the other had been asked. Neither came. They could not meet even under the roof of a stranger, and I had to content myself with profuse apologies from their followers, of whom a considerable number were present. So much for royal etiquette among the ruling classes of the swarthy population of Africa.

In architecture, utensils, weapons of war, implements of husbandry, dress, and mode of life, there is little difference between one tribe and another, but fashions in cut and colour of attire change frequently, and the same fashion is not observed among many tribes at the same time. One tribe adorns all garments with beads, another with buttons, a third with shells, bits of wood, or brass wire, all of which may be reversed in a few years. The hair is often worn so as to indicate the tribe to which a man belongs, and a royal messenger sent home with cropped hair would be equivalent to a declaration of war. The houses are all circular. A basket frame-work, about sixteen feet in diameter, forms the foundation, and this, daubed with clay over its lower part, and thatched with rough grass and reeds, serves as a palace for royalty and as shelter for the poorest serf. There is nothing to distinguish the houses of the rich from those of the poorest, nor do the internal arrangements differ in any essential in the case of persons of different rank. A few mats, a milk skin, calabash, assagais, a clay or cast-iron pot, a wooden basin, spoons, a grinding-stone for corn, drinking vessels made of the rind of the common gourd, pipes, walking sticks, and a skin pouch, constitute the entire furniture of the palace and the cottage. With these and a blanket, often of skin, for the men, and a petticoat and tipet, also of skin, for the women, an African establishment is set up and well supplied. The ruler of tens of thousands of the finest men physically, has a kit more slender than is required by the cragsmen of St. Kilda. The latter must add to the meagre stock of necessaries a stout rope of hemp or plaited hide; the African, living an easier life and under more genial skies, can dispense with almost all that we deem necessary for human existence and comfort, and he is perfectly contented and happy without them. He has never known them; does not know of their existence, and has no wish to be other than he is and has always been.

From earliest years the African is the slave of custom. When a child is born the mother is secluded for a month, reckoned by lunar time, and this period of seclusion is called *incubation*. If omitted, fecundity would cease. After the birth of the child, and the wise women have reported favourably, the father slaughters an animal—sheep, goat, or ox—as a thank-offering to the spirits of his ancestors, which are his household gods. If this domestic sacrifice should be neglected, and the child grow up sickly, it is attributed to the displeasure of the ancestors, and the magicians are called. They, after much ceremony and performance of mystic rites, order certain sacrifices to be offered to appease the spirits, and after days of feasting take their departure. The father is not subjected to seclusion or any other special ceremony beyond offering the sacrifices prescribed by custom.

When the child is about ten days old the hut is decorated with green branches. A number of sweet smelling herbs are collected, and a fire made of aromatic tomboti wood at the north side of the hut. The mother then—there being only women present—holds the child over the smoke, swaying it to and fro. When the child cries the mother says, "There goes the thief." The meaning is that the evil spirits are supposed to escape from the child during this ceremony. The same performance is gone through at intervals during the period of incubation by the wise women in attendance. The smoking process ensures mental vigour, wisdom, valour, strategy, and eloquence of speech. The spirit of fire escapes in smoke, and this the child receives and retains if the ceremony is performed by duly qualified persons. When the child is held over the fire for the last time, a number of cattle are collected outside the hut, and prayers are offered to the spirits the while. The first beast that makes water is the one selected by the spirits as a sacrifice, and it is slaughtered accordingly. Nor are such ceremonies confined to the child; the mother, before it is born, has to observe certain customs. She must at intervals partake of a drug prepared from a plant called the *belekani*, and the vessel used must be carefully hidden, so that no one may see it except herself and the magician who prescribes. Without this mode of treatment the child would be still-born. The lungs and liver of the animal slaughtered are hung in the hut, and some of the fat burned, as an offering to the spirits. A vessel filled with blood is placed at the side nearest the north, and the bearer of it says as he puts it down, "Eat now, ye gods, and be filled." The assembled crowd shout, "It is well said," and after much carousal disperse to their homes. The following day the person who prepared the drugs and food for the mother ties a string with charms round her neck, after which she goes to the river for water. There she takes a stone and casts it into a pool, and, addressing the spirits, says, "What are you looking at? Do not look at me," and casting in a second stone, fills her pitcher and returns home, carrying it on her head. She must not spill a drop of water, nor steady the pitcher with her hand. On her return she subjects the child to certain ceremonies. She first spits upon it all over, and then squirts milk from her breast into its eyes, ears, nostrils, &c. When this is done she resumes her normal mode of life, only that she has to perform the daily ceremonies in connection with the growth and development of her child.

Children are not killed or maimed, except in the case of a man who has fallen in war, and whose wife is taken by his nearest kinsman. The first-born is killed. It was the child of the assegai. When a widow marries her first child is killed.[1] If it were not, the husband would surely die. In all domestic relations the father is supreme, and the children are surnamed after him, and belong to his tribe. Neither father nor mother can transfer children to another clan, and adoption is unknown, except in the sense of foster parents, which is common. Names are selected in the most arbitrary manner, and any passing event may serve to suggest a name. A father who is a stoker calls his son "Engine;" a navvy names the heir of his house "Railway;" while a stevedore's labourer regards "Winch" as the most euphonious appellation he can bestow upon his first-born.

The life of an African may be said to begin at puberty, and the ceremonies that are connected with initiation into manhood and womanhood are both protracted and elaborate. Young men are initiated into the privileges of manhood, after undergoing the rites of circumcision. Young women pass, at a corresponding period of life, through the ceremonies connected with what the natives term *intonjane*. Circumcision is performed between the sixteenth and

---

[1] This practice is discontinued among all the tribes of the extreme south.

eighteenth year, and this being regarded as a most important rite, it is performed with much ceremony and circumstance of mystic practice.

At the season of the year when the crops are beginning to show signs of ripening, all the young men of a locality are circumcised by the village doctor or medicine man, magicians being always in attendance, and are then isolated in huts, previously prepared, at some distance from the ordinary dwellings. Men are appointed to watch over the neophytes, and to prevent their having intercourse with others, especially with women. The young men are daubed all over with a pure white clay, which, for the period of probation, is their distinguishing badge. During the months of probation, varying from two to six, they are subjected to many privations. If they can steal sheep, goat, or ox, they are at liberty to do so; but should a foray prove fruitless, they are beaten unmercifully for their clumsiness. If successful, their conduct is regarded as deserving of all praise. They are compelled to do violent bodily exercise in dancing and running, are often kept awake for several consecutive nights, beaten with saplings over the arms and thighs, and at intervals deprived of food for varying periods, all of which is meant to harden them, and render them indifferent to toil, privation, and pain. That a good many die in the training is a minor detail.

At the close of the initiatory training the white clay is washed off their bodies, each receives a new skin blanket, and they all repair to the residence of the head of the clan, where the councillors of the tribe have already assembled. Their bodies are now anointed with oil, and smeared over with red ochre. Harangues from the elders, minister of war, magician, and tribal bard follow. They are told that now the white clay is washed off their bodies, they are no longer boys. The utensils, tools, and clothing used during their isolation are burned along with their temporary huts, and the elders, dwelling on this, point out that all that belonged to boyhood must be of the past, and reappear no more in their lives. They are now men. Men's work is to be theirs. The duties of childhood, herding, hoeing, and ordinary drudgery, is to devolve in future on their younger brothers. At this stage arms are placed in their hands, as the sign of full manhood and its rights. With these they are to defend their chief, avenge his wrongs, wage war at his word, and generally use their weapons as he directs, even if against their own mothers; and this extreme of fidelity is occasionally demanded, as we shall see. There is no tattooing, knocking out of teeth, or malformation connected with the rites of circumcision. These are practised often as a matter of personal choice or adornment, but not otherwise. Among Zulus and Pondos the ears of boys and girls are pierced and distended, so as to admit a very thick quill. This is intended as a receptacle for ornaments, in the form of huge ear-rings or small tapering horn-shaped reeds, which hang dependent over both shoulders, the points looking forward and upwards, the reed being fixed in the lobe of the ear as if in a socket.

Girls are at puberty grouped and isolated in the same manner as boys. The rites connected with this period of life are too obscene in their nature to admit of details. The scientific reader will find a full account, written by the author of this book, in the "Journal of the Anthropological Institute."

South Africans are all polygamists, and many of their marriage customs are both peculiar and interesting. A man is free to marry a woman of his own or any other tribe, but there must be no blood-relationship between them. The precise degrees of consanguinity are not very clearly defined, but a man or woman whose origin can be traced to a common ancestor cannot be legally married. A man obtains a wife by giving her father a certain number of cattle. This, though often called such, is not purchase in the usual sense of the word. The woman does not become a chattel. She cannot be resold or ill-treated beyond well-defined legal limits. She retains certain rights to property and an interest in the cattle paid for her. They are a guarantee for the husband's good behaviour. If she is ill-treated or dismissed from her husband's house without good cause publicly proven, the cattle revert to her as her portion. Should the wife desert her home without good and sufficient cause, the husband claims the cattle and both they and their increase must be restored to him.

There are no special ceremonies necessary before marriage in the case of either bride or bridegroom, nor are the customs the same in all tribes. The choice of a wife seldom lies with the bridegroom in the case of a first wife, and the bride is never, under any circumstances, allowed to choose her own husband, as is the case among the natives of Torres Straits. The parents of eligible young people take the matter into consideration and talk it over. They discuss the advantages a marriage between the young folk would bring to them, and when the necessary preliminaries are satisfactorily arranged, the young man's father informs him that it is settled that so and so is to be his wife. He may have had other ambitions, and may never have seen his intended bride, nor even heard her name, but he is, as a rule, too wise to offer any serious opposition. By so doing, he is "throwing ashes" on the head of his parent, and running a risk of being consigned to the care and tuition of some old woman till he has learned better manners, and how to respect his seniors and forefathers. In the case of a "chief wife," the bridegroom may not see her, seldom does if a man of tribal standing, till after the marriage ceremonies are over. Greater latitude is allowed in the case of subordinate wives.

When the families have agreed upon the union, and after preliminary feasting and dancing at her home, the bride starts on her journey, going by easy stages and accompanied by her bridesmaids and attendants, the number being strictly regulated by the rank of the parties. On the morning preceding the marriage, the bride, accompanied by a number of girls with painted faces and clad in goat skins, makes her way towards the bridegroom's kraal, and when within a convenient distance of it, halts. The bride then sings a song. After she has ceased singing, a sheep or goat is sent from the kraal for her acceptance. This is called by them, "Taking down from the mount." If her party are satisfied with the present, they advance at once; if not, the singing is resumed and a second animal is sent. This has the desired effect, and the party approach the dwelling, where mutual salutations and compliments are exchanged. The bridal party then retire, and spend the next night dancing and feasting.

The following morning, the bride prepares herself to receive her husband. All the men of the neighbourhood gather, wearing no garments except what nature has supplied. Each drives his best racing ox before him. He carries a shield on his shoulder and an assagai poised in his right hand. As he advances, he sings the praises of his forefathers and recounts their deeds of valour. These guests surround the bride's party who begin to sing and dance, advancing gradually towards the bridegroom's kraal. He stands, *in puris naturalibus*, to receive his bride, and when the dance is finished, she is conducted to the house she is to occupy. There she adorns herself with circlets of beadwork and flowers, and distributes smaller ones among her maids of honour. The day closes with an ox race—an institution peculiar to Africa—dancing, feasting, and merry-making. Presents are made by the bridegroom to his mother-in-law, and she also receives a fat ox, which is solely for the use of her female friends. The bride's praises and virtues are sung by the women, and a fire having been kindled by one of the bridesmaids in her house, the formal ceremonies are brought to a close.

All these ceremonies are closely observed, and any violation of customary usage is, even when unintentional, visited with the severest punishment. The following incident recorded by the Hon. Charles Brownlee, than whom there is no greater living authority on native manners, illustrates the jealousy with which such customs are guarded, especially in the case of persons of rank. Mr. Brownlee says :—

"About this time, one evening, a young Zulu soldier came to the mission-house in great distress. He informed the missionaries, Messrs. Champion and Grout, that a few days previously, he and a companion were travelling to head-quarters to join their regiment; that at one village where they stayed, they went to the *ilawu* (the traveller's hut); that he there took a mat, and on unrolling it found that it contained bead ornaments and articles of female dress, such as are used only by the royal family. Seeing this, he again rolled up the mat and put it aside. It belonged to a girl of the king's harem, on her way to the capital, who had stayed there with other girls and attendants on the previous night. She had forgot her mat and ornaments. On arriving at head-quarters, he was at once detailed for cattle guard, but on his return, in the evening, he was met by a young man of his regiment, who told him that his companion had been put to death for touching the mat and ornaments of the king's children, and that he himself was to be put to death. He had, therefore, fled for his life, and as he feared that the pursuers were close after him, he begged the missionaries to conceal him in their house. They informed him that concealment in the house could be of no possible avail, and could afford him no safety, and that, besides, the missionaries would, by this act, be compromising themselves. It was, however, suggested that he should cross the Tugela, and make his escape into Natal. His reply was, 'I have already been to the Tugela. It is flooded. I cannot swim, and if I could, escape is impossible for the river is full of crocodiles. Hide me even in one of your boxes till the river is passable.'

"Here, indeed, was a sad and perplexing case, but our perplexity was soon ended by three men taking off the unfortunate youth, for a girl named Mbikicane, who was at the mission-house, having overheard the story of the poor soldier, went at once and told her father Uxam, who arrested the man. The matter being reported to Dingan, he sent orders for the execution of the poor fellow, and three or four days after, I heard some boys with great glee describing the manner of the execution, which appeared to afford them infinite amusement."

After marriage a man has to be very reserved in the presence of his mother-in-law, whom he must not address except when absolutely necessary. The bride must not address her father-in-law, except when veiled, under any pretext. The time during which these restraints are imposed varies according to the rank of those interested, from a few weeks to many months, or till there are children of the marriage, when the normal manner of life is resumed. There is no restraint between other relations, as brothers and sisters, cousins, or brothers and sisters-in-law.

In connection with marriage ceremonies, the magician is not necessarily in attendance, nor even consulted; but in cases of illness and death, his services are indispensable, and it is in this connection that witchcraft and superstition assume their most abhorrent forms. With the exception of natural decay, the result of old age and infirmity, disease and death is almost invariably attributed to witchcraft. It is acknowledged that men are born with disease in their constitution, the result of the spirits having been displeased at some action done by the parents or by one of them. This may lead to death, and the cause cannot be explained. It is like scab in sheep, which is supposed to be a natural defect in the animal—this opinion is held by the more ignorant Dutch Boers, and for which nothing can be done. It is accounted for by referring it to that convenient region, the ancestral spirit world.

But this is very exceptional, and, when a case of sickness occurs, the medicine man is called, who prescribes certain remedies which are jealously guarded as a secret of the healing art. Many of these herbalists have acquired considerable skill in treating common ailments. Among the plants from which they draw their supplies, the common aloe, the castor oil plant, nux vomica, rhubarb, fern root—*aspidium filix-mas*, acacia bark, and many others might be cited. If a cure is effected, the whole affair ends with the offering of a domestic sacrifice. Should the prescribed remedies fail, and the patient either get worse or continue without marked change, the magicians are called, and their treatment is as irrational and empirical as the medicine man's is sensible and in accordance with reason. If they determine that the disease is the result of some slight or offence given to the ancestors, a sacrifice is offered to appease their wrath. The bones and fat of the victims are carefully collected and burned. As the smoke ascends, the magician, assuming the priestly character, prays, thus: "Ye who are above, who have gone before, look upon us in pity, and remove our affliction. Ye, who see it is not the dead we offer, hear. It is blood. We repent. Will you not relent and be favourable to us who offer sacrifice to you now." A rich reward awaits the magicians in the event of recovery, and there the case ends.

If the disease happens to be the work of wizards or witches—the magicians determine its nature by occult communication with the spirit world, an entirely different course of treatment is necessary. After the patient has been examined, and his history, or as much as shall serve the purpose, ascertained, the following may be taken as a characteristic method of treatment:—A small portion of the skin, generally behind the shoulders, is rubbed by a stone or other rough substance, till it is slightly abraded, but not bleeding. Then a prepared horn is applied, the magician sucking the smaller end and forming a partial vacuum under it. The abraded surface bleeds slightly, and, on removing the horn, he searches, or pretends to search the accumulated blood for the cause of the disorder, and presently starts to his feet with an ant, beetle, gnat, or other insect in his hand, exclaiming, "There is the disease for you; it is now extracted; the patient shall do well." When improvement follows, and the hopes of the patient do much, the magician is rewarded, and takes his departure, after having given various dark hints about the wizard who originated the malady, but these are of Delphic ambiguity.

If there should be no improvement, or the patient dies, the magician in that case has to discover the author of the evil. This department of the art is known as "smelling out," and may be best considered under magic, and divination, of which I shall have something to say in its proper place.

When a chief or other great man dies, men are appointed to watch the body till the whole tribe can be assembled for the funeral. An opening is then made in the side of the house. The corpse is bound up in the leopard skin which was the late chief's robe of office, and is then brought out by the newly-made opening, never by the door. The warriors, standing in order to their arms, give the royal salute as if the chief were still alive and reviewing his troops. A grave is prepared at the gate of the cattle fold, a new entrance being made for the cattle, and that over the grave closed. The body, wrapped in the royal robe, is then deposited in a space hollowed out under the bank on one side of the grave, and the opening built up, after which the earth is filled in as usual. The ornaments, rings, armlets, anklets, tobacco pipes, and articles of apparel worn by the departed are placed in the grave, as well as his broken spear, walking stick, and other personal effects. When all is finished, the multitude once more stand in order, and, bowing low towards the grave, repeat three times, "Chief! fare thee well," and then depart in silence. Fasting, as a semi-religious ordinance, is not uncommon on such occasions, and may be continued for two whole days or even longer. On the death of a chief, the men shave their heads in token of mourning. In the case of ordinary men, only his relatives shave.

After the funeral, men are appointed to watch over the grave, day and night, for several years, to prevent wizards exhuming the chief's body, and using portions of it for the purposes of their dark art. Formerly it was customary to bury chiefs only; now sepulture is universal, except in cases of death by lightning and other accidents. Persons who touch a dead body are unclean, and must bathe in running water before associating with other men or partaking of food. The ghost of the departed is not feared as such; it simply goes to join the ancestral spirits, and this is "going home." The widow is secluded for a brief period, and casts away all her old clothing. After she has obtained new garments, she may be visited, and resumes her ordinary life. The same grave is never used more than once, and any one touching the bones of the dead would be polluted, and require protracted treatment at the hands of the priests, which would include isolation, washings, and sacrifice.

When all the funeral rites are completed, and the mourners have dispersed to their homes, the house occupied by the deceased at the time of his death is burned with all that it contains. Even articles of value, grain, utensils, arms, ornaments, beds, bedding and furniture, all must be destroyed by fire. They are polluted by the presence of the dead in the house and cannot be cleansed, nor would it be permissible to use them in any case on pain of the dire displeasure of the ancestors. Articles removed from the house before a man dies may be used. Into every relation of life this quasi ancestor worship enters. Domestic events, war, peace, agriculture, disease among cattle and goats, drought, floods, cold, heat, pestilence, sterility, fecundity, and almost every circumstance that affects the life of man, is traced to spirit influence, and as the ancestors are pleased or displeased events are propitious or the reverse.

It is impossible to understand African domestic life without some acquaintance with their system of law, and especially how that affects property and inheritance. The chief holds the land for communal purposes, and each member of the tribe cultivates as much as he requires. During the time a man occupies and uses land it is regarded as his own, and no one, not even his chief, can dispossess him without compensation. At his death his ground passes to his heir, but he can neither will nor otherwise dispose of it to any other. Should he, during his lifetime, give another a portion of it, this is regarded as a loan and does not in any sense interfere with the heir's rights. A man's land cannot be put under arrest or taken possession of for debt or any form of liability while he remains a member of the tribe. For certain crimes, murder, arson, theft, witchcraft, overt acts leading to war, &c., he can be expelled the community, and if taken in the act may be slain with impunity. He is a wolf.

A large portion of arable land is always reserved for younger sons, and for men joining the tribe from time to time. This is allotted by the chief. It is never in one block, but in strips and patches scattered all over the locations. Africans of to-day send no colonies of new arrivals to a specially reserved Goshen to increase and multiply, while they retain their nationality, and in the end become a troublesome or dangerous factor. The policy is rather that they should be fused into, and amalgamate with the general tribal community.

The grazing lands are the common property of the tribe, and each man can pasture his herds and flocks where his fancy may lead him. By common consent and courtesy, the vicinity of the "great-place" is reserved specially for the chief's cattle. It may also be noticed that the "great-place" is never near cultivated land. The chief's cattle are not supposed to be disturbed by such vulgar beings as herd boys, which would happen if pastured on lands adjoining corn fields and ordinary homesteads. At the chief's farm homesteads, of which he has several, lands are cultivated as at ordinary dwellings.

Besides land used for arable and pastoral purposes, we almost invariably find, before the advent of Europeans, huge stretches of forest and plain reserved for the purposes of the chase. On these high lying grounds the game is left undisturbed, except during the winter or hunting season. Hunts are then organised on a great scale, and continued for many days at a time. On such expeditions hundreds of men and dogs accompany the chief. The ordinary warrior's spear—assegai—is the only weapon. I, of course, speak of the custom before the introduction of fire-arms, and the unwritten law is, that to him who first draws blood, however insignificant the scratch, belongs the quarry. The animals of the chase comprise what is usually termed the large game of Africa. I am not aware that natives succeeded in killing full-grown elephants before they became acquainted with fire-arms. A lion they hardly attack, unless he is old and lazy, and becomes very troublesome about their homesteads. Whole villages have been known to migrate to avoid a place where lions had taken up their quarters.

Before entering on a hunting expedition the dogs are dosed with medicine to ensure success. Men are not dosed, but the organiser of the hunt prepares a quantity of snuff. This he distributes among those who are to take part in the expedition. He presents it to them with his right hand and they must accept with the right also; otherwise ill-luck would attend them. The manner of inviting men to a hunt is peculiar. The messenger goes from kraal to kraal but does not enter any house, nor does he utter a word. He simply lies down and begins to imitate the movements of some well known wild animal. When this is observed, the villagers begin to pelt him with cow dung, asking where the meet is to take place and when. He mentions time and place, and takes his departure to the next village. Before he has completed his rounds he is bespattered from head to foot with cow dung, and in this plight he returns home. Certain unimportant ceremonies are observed in the field, such as plucking out the right eye of any game killed and pouring medicine, which has been charmed by magicians, into the socket. Men do not eat wild pigs, hares, fish, ducks, geese, turkeys, or domestic fowls, but all of them, fish excepted, may be eaten by women and children, and are frequently hunted and killed by men for the use of their families. Deer of all kinds, antelopes and many wild birds, may be eaten by all. Fish is never eaten; it belongs to the category of reptiles which are shunned and abhorred.

To return to the question of property, we find that the law of inheritance, though at first apparently a mass of confusion, is better defined than any other branch of jurisprudence. When a man has but one wife his eldest son is his heir, and inherits all his civil and material rights as a tribesman. He is also entitled to a certain proportion of all movable property. The residue may be divided between other members of the family in any proportions. Daughters can thus inherit, though in practice this seldom happens. They are supposed to get married and add to the father's wealth, and when past the ordinary age of marriage, are regarded as a failure, and become little better than domestic slaves, or so much useless lumber. Theirs is a hard lot. When there are more wives than one the position is complicated by a variety of regulations. The first wife may not be, and seldom is, the chief wife. It is the latter's eldest son who is the heir, but at the same time the first wife's eldest son has a claim superior to that of other sons of subordinate wives. During the father's lifetime he usually apportions his property to the respective households, always subject to the heir's claims, and any property not so apportioned is equally divided, the heir taking the largest share according to a recognised ratio. When a man has no son, he can will his movable property to other than relatives, subject to a claim which his brother, if his mother's son, has. His civil rights lapse, and revert to the chief in whose gift they are to confer on whom he will. When a man dies both childless and intestate, his brother, if his mother's son, is the heir-at-law, or failing such brother, then the nephew. If he had no full brothers, then the one of his father's sons highest in rank by other wives is the heir, and takes all the rights which would belong to a full brother. The wife's relations do not inherit, nor do the daughters or sisters of the deceased in an intestate estate, nor under any circumstances other than the very rare cases already referred to.

In their ordinary home life men are waited upon by women and eat apart. The only reason that can be given for this custom is the subordinate position assigned to woman, who practically, though not legally, becomes a chattel after marriage, and whose duty it is to attend upon her husband and his friends, receiving such signs of favour as may be bestowed on her with due thankfulness. To act otherwise involves the taking of another wife, who for the time being becomes the favourite.

In times of great plenty the men take the principal meal of the day about 11 o'clock A.M., in public. A little before that time each man in the village sends what has been prepared for him to some shady or sheltered spot, and then all saunter slowly to the appointed place, where they sit and talk, taking their meal very leisurely, and frequently exchanging portions when different articles have been prepared for them. The women sit in their respective huts, and any man or woman who, through accident or as a stranger, has no food, shares in whatever is going. They are, however, supposed to be fed by the head of the village. It is he alone who is responsible for hospitality, and to such an extent is it carried that food at meal time may almost be said to be common property. The same tub or basin is used to hold the food of a considerable number of persons. Each lifts a portion with a large spoon, eating it with the aid of his fingers. Giving a stranger a separate vessel apart from the family basin would be regarded as an insult. It is supposed to indicate fear of some contagious disease, such as leprosy.

The ordinary articles of food are, maize, millet, pumpkins, beans, milk, and the flesh of animals. Certain articles are unclean and are never eaten, while others are unclean to men but not to women and children. Blood is never used as an article of food, but the blood of both men and animals enters into magician's decoctions and war medicine. There is no cannibalism in South Africa. In former times the Basutos did undoubtedly eat human flesh, but in what connection tradition does not make clear; most likely enemies slain in war. Prisoners seem to have always been retained as domestic drudges. The flesh of the lion and also that of the spotted leopard is at times cooked and eaten by warriors to make them courageous. The practice is not general though found among all the tribes. Portions of these animals are used by magicians in the preparations they administer to warriors before going to war, but these are not the only superstitions which cluster round the history of Africans in their unequal struggle with the pale-faced intruder.

About the year 1857 certain of the South African tribes became possessed by an extraordinary delusion. I refer to it partly to show the nature of their superstitious beliefs, chiefly to show the power possessed by the magicians. Shortly before the date referred to there had been a good deal of guerrilla warfare between the English settlers and the native tribes, resulting in confiscation of territory. Under this the natives smarted, and cast about for a means of revenge. In previous wars they had been heavily handicapped by the necessity of guarding their cattle in comparatively open country, where cavalry could operate with effect. An impostor, named Umlanjeni, predicted that if the confederate tribes slaughtered all their cattle, destroyed every pit of corn, and left the ground untilled in the spring, that at a given time their ancestors would rise and drive the English into the sea, whence they came. He further alleged that he saw in his visions the cattle belonging to the ancestors coming in huge droves over the hills, and that, after the expulsion of the English, every man could have as many as he had provided folds for before the arrival of the eventful day. The corn-pits also were to be filled without tillage.

This delusion took possession of their fevered

imaginations, and a number of tribes destroyed every hoof and left their corn lying in heaps to rot. Feasting, dancing, and war-like demonstrations occupied their whole time. In vain the Government tried to avert the impending ruin. Nothing could be done but await the development of events, and prepare for war. Before the arrival of the eventful day, which happened to be the morning after full moon, solemn fasts were appointed and observed. Every hill smoked with sacrifices offered to the ancestors, and, on the evening preceding the resurrection day, a solemn service was held under a hill near the mouth of the Great Kei River, at which tens of thousands of expectant men were present. The sign given by Umlanjeni was that on the morning succeeding the full moon the sun was to rise double. During that memorable night not an eye closed. Young men feasted, drank, danced, and carried on high revelry, while the older sat in silent groups, or walked anxiously about the huge fold prepared for the risen cattle of their chiefs. As the night wore on and all things remained silent and still, under the bright moon and feebly shining stars, the anxiety deepened till the dawn of day proclaimed the sun's returning once more. As the king of day showed the edge of his disk above the horizon all eyes were turned to the east. Slowly and majestically he rose, but his companion lagged behind, and already black fear entered hearts which a little ago beat high with hope and expectation. Umlanjeni declared that they had mistaken the day of the full moon, and predicted triumph on the morrow. The next twenty-four hours was but a sad time. Such food as had not been destroyed was quite exhausted, and as afternoon wore to evening hunger reminded them of their possible plight, should Umlanjeni's predictions prove false. But not a murmur was heard till once more the sun appeared in solitary majesty. After this it was in vain that skilled and daring warriors urged their men to follow them in a bold rush on the Colony, if but to secure food for a perishing nation. Along the frontier every pass was securely guarded, nor were hungry and dispirited men likely to force them. What followed is ordinary history, with which, in these pages, I have nothing to do, nor with this delusion, except as illustrating the magician's power, and the manner in which a semi-savage, though brave people, may be lured to their doom.

Before a tribe goes to war great meetings are held, and after the decision of the council is made known the warriors must be prepared for active service. The war minister determines the strength of the army that is to take the field, and the men are selected by sub-chiefs, a certain proportion always remaining at home. It is the province of the war doctor to prepare the soldiers for the march, and this he does by incantations, sprinkling, war-paint, and cursing of their enemies. The chief, too, takes an active part in these preliminaries. He orders the men to provide themselves with shields, and those who have oxen must kill them when their skins are fancied by the warriors. They receive compensation in kind from the captured cattle after the war is over. Skins of wild cats, monkeys, rats, moles, and other creatures are in great demand for personal adornment, and the feathers of the crested crane fetch fabulous prices at such times.

Scouts are sent into the enemies' country to procure portions of the hair from the tails of their cattle, and also a quantity of cow dung from their folds. These the doctor uses to bewitch the enemy, and to prevent their cattle running to the ordinary cry, as in racing—all cattle are trained to run to a certain cry, so that they can easily be removed to a distance in time of danger. After this the army is assembled, and war dances are held at intervals while the process of " doctoring " proceeds. The ceremonies are usually as follows :—The warriors form a ring and sing certain songs, which are never sung, and must on no account be sung, by women. As the singing dies away dancing begins, and is continued till the men are nearly exhausted ; the exercise being very violent, this is not very long. The chief is meantime sitting alone, and the braves call out at intervals as they dance and caper, " What are you keeping us here for ? You are a coward. Turn us out. Lead us if you dare." The chief next commands them to sing their national or tribal song, after which the man who is recognised as the bravest in the army performs a dance before him, and sings the praises of the chief and his ancestors.

This concludes the review, and the chief addresses his men something to this effect:—" The young man "— a contemptuous mode of speaking of an enemy— " despises me, and I am going to take you to him. His cattle are already mine; they are in my hands." The last reference is to the hair collected by the scouts, which he holds in his hand.

The whole army then marches to the nearest stream or river, and the doctor, standing on the bank—up stream—throws in some charmed medicine, on which the whole body plunge headlong into the water. After bathing they return again to the great place. On their arrival there the chiefs of clans are called forward, and receive a powder from the war doctor. Four men of each clan then advance to their respective chiefs, and are given some of the powder. They then proceed to doctor the troops. This is done by making a small incision above the right eye, into which the powder is rubbed. They are next sprinkled by the priest, and return to their homes, where they must remain three days. On the day of final muster there is a further ceremony performed by the tribal priests, after which all begin singing war songs and shouting defiance at the enemy. The chief pretends to weep, and then the braves come forward to comfort him, but he cries out, " Away! you are a lot of cowards. It was only my father who was a chief; it was only your fathers who did great deeds for him. Oh! what a degradation it is for me to be in command of such a lot of cowards." By degrees he is comforted, and tells them they are to fight as did their fathers, and only to return when laden with spoil. When it is nearly dawn, the chief issues his final orders, and says, "Men, to-day I do not want cattle. You may capture for yourselves. All I want is a young calf." All the same, when the division of the spoil is made he picks out the best and fattest. A great chief never goes into action; he remains apart, surrounded by his bodyguard. When cattle are captured—all war in Africa resolves itself into a cattle hunt—the fattest animal is killed and eaten raw. While in the enemy's country soldiers must not wash except with medicine, or rather with water, to which medicine has been added by magicians. On the return of the expedition brave warriors are rewarded, the cattle are divided, the doctor handsomely feed, and all disperse to their homes, as if nothing had happened.

Enemies slain in war are not, as a rule, mutilated, though this may happen. The war doctor may order any noted enemy slain to be decapitated. The skull is cleaned and made into a bowl for holding war medicine, with which he sprinkles the army, and the medicine from this novel cup is supposed to convey to the warriors something of the courage and virtues of the original owner. Portions of the slain are used in making decoctions by magicians.

The following, from the conversation of a Gaika named Go, a most intelligent man, who was attached to the staff of the Hon. Charles Brownlee, who records the incident, will serve to illustrate certain of their war practices. He says :—

"Go was my constant attendant. At night by the camp fire Go would begin : 'Well, in the last war I was in the Colony. Two other men accompanied me. We went to see what we could pick up from the Fingoes. We went to Alice, but the Fingoes were on the alert, and we could get nothing. I crept up to their camp fire, when one of their diviners was performing an incantation against the Gaikas. He had the dried fingers of a dead man in his hand, and was shouting and dancing about in the most frantic manner, predicting victory and success to the Fingoes, and pronouncing an incantation against Sandili, saying, 'Little jackal of the Gaikas, get out of this.' The people shouted the refrain, '*Siyavuma!*' *i.e.*, 'We assent.' On the following morning I fell in with the Gaika army, under command of Oba, on their way to Alice to capture the Fingoe cattle. Two ospreys had, in the morning, flown over the army, uttering piercing shrieks. This the older men considered a bad omen, and they begged Oba to allow the army to return and be re-charmed, as when that kind of bird flew over an army it boded defeat, and indicated that the bird was there to feast on the eyes of the slain; but Oba was determined to proceed, and would not be terrified by the shrieks of birds. The chief was young and obstinate, and he would listen to no one. This was the first time he was in command, and it should not be said that he was afraid of either Fingoes or birds. The order to advance was given, and Qwarana, a brave warrior, was appointed to lead. As we came to the crest of the hill, and in sight of Alice, we saw the Fingoe cattle below us. Six Fingoe scouts on foot were between the cattle and us, but instead of fleeing with the cattle, they sent them to Alice in charge of the herd boys, and advanced towards us, shouting '*Basoliwe*,' meaning,

'They are cursed,' referring to the previous night's incantation. When they had come quite near to us, they fired a volley, shooting Qwarana through the body. This checked our advance, and Qwarana was led back by two men, who supported him on his horse, which was covered with blood. This was enough for the waverers. They turned and fled, and although at this time only the six Fingoes were opposed to us, the panic became general. Oba did all in his power to stay the flight. He prayed and begged the Gaikas to act like men; he called them cowards and women; he broke the heads of his flying men; but it was of no avail, he might as well have tried to stop the course of this stream after a thunderstorm."

Oba, headstrong as he was brave, led a somewhat chequered life, but to the end of his days he remained a fine specimen of the Gaika of a past generation. I knew him in his old age when he occupied a paltry Government location, and often thought how bitter his feelings must have been, when he contrasted his actual position with his prospects in early life, as heir to one of the most powerful chieftainships in South Africa.

In Zululand, not only are all the institutions of the country influenced by their military system, but even the domestic relations of the people are greatly modified since its introduction, now more than a hundred years ago. The military organisation adopted by Chaka—the first real monarch of Zululand—was not a native product. It was introduced in this way:—Dingiswayo, chief of the Umtetwa, was an exile in the Cape Colony, and was present at an action where a mere handful of disciplined men scattered several thousands of armed savages. Shortly thereafter he returned to his own country, where he was welcomed and reinstated in power. His first care was to organise an army on the European model, and Chaka, who was in turn a fugitive from Zululand, served as a private in Dingiswayo's army. When Chaka returned to Zululand on the death of his father, he improved upon his teacher's military system, and organised the most perfect savage army that ever took the field against an enemy.

He carried on a war of extermination against all neighbouring tribes. Thousands fell under the Zulu spears, and tens of thousands, driven to the mountains, perished of starvation. The country for hundreds of miles was made a desert, and the whole of what is now the Colony of Natal was a hunting preserve from which the inhabitants had been driven or killed.

The system of government which was introduced by Chaka was most cruel and arbitrary. Death was the penalty for all offences real or imaginary. The offence of the head of a household might involve the death of the whole family, and that of a head-man the death of all his adherents. Any one cognisant of an offence, and who did not report it, suffered the same penalty as the offenders. This dreadful system of tyranny was carried out through the instrumentality of an army which, during the reign of Dingan, numbered forty thousand men, all eager to be employed, in order that promotion for bravery or fidelity might be obtained, and what was of equal importance, that the young soldiers might imitate their seniors in being able to narrate deeds of blood.

Distinguished bravery was always brought to the king's notice, and was usually rewarded by promotion or a share of the spoil, while cowardice or incapacity was punished with the utmost barbarity. Three generals were, under Chaka, deprived of their eyesight, and left to starve, no one daring to feed them, because the divisions under their command, in an expedition towards Delagoa Bay, had lost their way, and many of the soldiers had died of fever. The fiat of the ruthless savage was, " Your eyes have been of no use to you in my service; they are therefore of no use whatever," and the unfortunate generals then and there had their eyes dug out with pointed stakes.

In 1837, Dingan sent out an army in three divisions for the purpose of exterminating the Swazies. Their instructions were that on a certain day they were to meet and cut off the Swazies from their strongholds on the Pongolo River. Mongo, whose division marched along the coast, got entangled in the extensive swamps and marshes of that region and arrived too late. The expedition failed of its object, and the other two generals having returned, Mongo was left to fight his way out alone. This he did with conspicuous skill and bravery, but nothing could avert the wrath of the king. Mr. Brownlee, who as a boy witnessed the return of Mongo's division, says of it :—

"On a lovely Sunday morning in June, Mongo's division appeared in sight of the capital. As it approached, short strains of war songs were heard, but died away almost as soon as they were begun. The army filed through the great gate in silence, up to the royal residence, Mongo at its head in plumes and shield and costly war dress, the gift of the king. Dingan sat in his great state chair, before an aromatic tomboti-wood fire, surrounded by many Zulu nobles. Mongo led the way, filed past before the king, and took his position to the right, but his salutation was not returned by either king or nobles. It was sad to see these weary and worn warriors falling into their position, and standing in silence while the division in detachments, with 6000 cattle, came filing past. Their numbers had no charm for the Zulu despot, he had failed in exterminating a tribe which might in time be rivals to the Zulus, and all was gall and wormwood to him. When the last man had taken his place, when the last cow had been consigned to the general herd, when the proud, plumed and shielded soldiers had in silence taken their places with downcast looks, like so many condemned criminals, Mongo was ordered to stand forward, and stood before the king, erect and tall, a magnificent savage, with shield reaching to his chin, and grasping a spear which had laid many a foeman low, at the behest of his sovereign. The scene to my boyish mind was awful, and when the king spoke it became terrible, for his words were the explosion of pent up rage. I remember the words as if they had been uttered only yesterday. 'Now Jogo'—Mongo's military title—'bird of the mountain, thorny-backed python, I have made you great. You are in charge of my royal home at Kangela.

I have given you an order. You have not performed it. You are therefore degraded. Your wives, children, and all your property are taken from you, and you are reduced to the lowest rank.' Jojo remained standing, erect and silent. He uttered no word of explanation, he pleaded no past services, well knowing the inexorable will of his tyrant master. Poor Jojo, it was a sad home-coming for him. Only one month before, he had gone forth as the proud commander of an army, now he returned a wretched outcast with neither wife, child, nor property, and from being viceroy of Kangela, he was reduced to the lowest rank."

Of the Information Department little need be said. During an expedition messengers were despatched by each general at short intervals to report the progress made. Many of these were intercepted and killed, but this mattered little ; human life was cheap. Of the fidelity required of an African soldier the following affords an illustration, where a brave man had to act as the executioner of his own mother.

Mdli at his death left two sons, full brothers, Mapopoma, a mere child, and Sigwebana, by Godase, his great wife. The former was as a boy a page in Dingan's household, and had afterwards a commission as Major in one of the regiments. Shortly after his promotion, a beautiful young woman of the King's harem visited Sigwebana's residence, her native place, for medical treatment. Dingan was not satisfied as to the cause of the home visits and consulted one of his magicians, whose oracular response was, " Is Sigwebana greater than the King? Why then do the King's children prefer Sigwebana to the King ?"

This was enough, and it was decided that Sigwebana and his family, and the young woman were to be put to death, the execution being intrusted to Sigwebana's own brother, Mapopoma. Sigwebana being a general favourite, he received private information of his impending fate, and at once made arrangements for flight to Natal under cover of night; but on arriving at the Tugela, he found his brother Mapopoma already there with a small detachment of his regiment. Sigwebana, his brother Timni, and a few other adherents, covered by their shields, cut their way through the opposing force. While this hand-to-hand conflict was proceeding, some of the men, women, and children, got across the Tugela, while Godase and others, in the darkness, returned to their homes which were about eight miles from the river. Mapopoma then sent to the capital to report what he had done, and to ask for instructions regarding the sympathisers with, and adherents of Sigwebana. The order was "All must die." Godase, being warned of her danger, fled with two female attendants to the mission-house, to seek shelter there, which was given to her. Early next morning six of Mapopoma's soldiers came to the station saying Godase was hidden there, and the missionaries were to bring her out. This they refused to do, and the soldiers rushed into the house and dragged out the unfortunate women. No female wails were heard ; no supplication for mercy ; no prayer for life. Godase said not a word. She stepped out as calmly as when she voluntarily submitted to a painful operation by Dr. Adams sometime before this. She saw that her hour was come, and she calmly faced her fate. She knew she might as well try to calm the raging wind, as to appeal to the feelings of Zulu soldiers, and the only manifestation of feeling was on the part of the missionaries, who in helpless agony, saw their best friend being led away to execution. At a little distance from the house, and, still in sight, the soldiers felled the passive helpless women with clubs, remarking that it was not necessary to kill the infants as the wolves would do that.

So perished Godase under the hand of the son she had so carefully brought up, and who was the pride of her old age. Such a system as this could not continue long. The hill of execution near the royal residence was never without carrion, and vultures sat patiently, day after day, on the trees waiting for fresh victims. These were felled with heavy clubs, and were often attacked by the vultures long before life was extinct. Repeated atrocities, and the uncertainty of human life, alarmed all parties, and in an unexpected hour the tyrant fell, as tyrants often do, by the hand of the assassin. A milder reign was introduced by Panda, but the old military despotism was re-established by Cetywayo, and continued till the Zulu power was finally overthrown by Sir Bartle Frere.

In Africa it is but a step from the warrior to the husbandman, and the soldier of to-day may be found peaceably following the plough to-morrow. If we except the Bushmen, all African tribes towards the south may be regarded as regular tillers of the soil. There are not many superstitions connected with the pursuit of agriculture. Among the Pondos nothing of the new crop may be eaten till after the chief has held the feast of first-fruits. When sowing seed it is mixed with bits of snake skin, and also small pieces of the skin of the ant bear are added. Along the coast there is a practice of scattering fine black sea sand, and the powdered root of a certain plant, over the outskirts of the fields. This is to avoid blight and hail. At the feast of first-fruits the cattle from the neighbourhood are collected and the bulls set to fight to determine which is to be the victor for the year. A great deal of noise and dancing goes on, and people are not supposed to be responsible for what they say or do. Should a man stab another he is free from blame, and even insults offered to the chief are not punished. At the close of this saturnalia the chief assembles the council and makes certain regulations for the year, which for the time being have in the tribe all the force of ancient law. Magicians are occasionally employed to exercise their arts in order to secure a rich harvest and to prevent the destruction of the growing crops by hail or blight. The ceremonies are not elaborate. The usual custom is to kindle a fire, and as the dense smoke of green branches and green corn stalks ascends, to throw in charms—shells, horse hair, leopard teeth, and other substances, and at the same time exorcise the demon of blight, hail, or drought. Another system is to fill a horn with special medicine and corn leaves. The magician then goes into the middle of the field where a small space has been cleared. Round this he walks, and taking mouthfuls of the medicine squirts it on the growing crop. When he has completed this squirting he shouts, "You are left now, make haste and grow." If insects are ravaging the crops, one is taken from each field and put into a gourd, which is then burned in a hole dug in the corn field. This is supposed to be effectual.

During the summer season hail showers are not uncommon, and when the appearance of the sky indicates the approach of a storm, the magicians, accompanied by all they can muster, repair to eminences near the dwellings. There they shout and yell in the most frantic manner to divert the storm from its course. Such storms frequently diverge from the straight line, and occasionally part into two or more sections in their course. This is attributed to the power of the magicians. He who has the highest skill diverts the storm from his own locality, and should he fail it is because one more powerful than he was working against him, and sent the storm on the course it took.

Most amusing incidents could be related in connection with this practice. One must suffice. The summer of 1885-86, was one during which hail storms were very prevalent. One day a very severe one passed near the writer's dwelling. All the magicians were out, and succeeded in diverting it to the next valley. On the following day an old magician came to me expecting to be complimented, when the following conversation took place.

"The white chief is indebted to us to-day. There would be no fruit in his garden if we had not gone out to meet the storm."

"May I ask where you sent the storm, and what valley suffered from its severity?"

"We turned the storm and sent it over to Ncolosi; it went as far west as the Bele."

"You are a curious doctor, you come and tell me that you have saved my garden from hail, and that you sent the storm to your own chief's great place. What will he say if I tell him this morning's conversation?"

A roar of laughter burst from the bystanders, and my friend, hiding his head in his blanket, fled precipitately leaving the white man for once master of the situation.

The religion of the Bantu, which they not only profess but really regulate their conduct by, is based on the belief that the spirits of their ancestors interfere constantly in their affairs, and is a curious mixture of magic, witchcraft and devotion. Every man worships his own ancestors and offers sacrifices to avert their wrath. The clan worships the spirits of the ancestors of its chiefs, and the tribe worships the spirits of the ancestors of the paramount chief.

When all the clans belonging to a tribe regard their chief as descended from a common ancestor, the belief welds the civil community and military organisation together; hence the coherence of the Zulu army as distinguished from almost any other African tribe. This element of union is wanting when the tribe is composed of clans of different origin. In such cases an able chief by nice balancing may keep them all well together, but there is always a disintegrating if not an explosive element present.

It is characteristic of Africans to drive all thoughts of the unseen world from their minds, and never mention it when it is possible to avoid it. Their greatest dread is to offend their ancestors and the only way to avoid this is to do everything according to traditional usage. To swear by the spirit of a departed chief is the most binding form of contract. Under such a system all progress is almost impossible. And when to this we add that any man who is mentally ahead of his fellows speedily earns the reputation of a wizard, for whom there is neither pity nor compassion, and whose end is generally a violent death, we can understand how matters have continued unchanged for thousands of years. We understand how in the short glinting time of peace and plenty that occasionally throws a beam of light and joy across his village gathering, we find the African dancing the same steps as are depicted in old wall paintings of ancient Egypt, the land of his captivity; steps which he danced round his chief's *pombi* pot before he was marched off with galled neck to take his place in the famous slave market of that country; steps which are the fashion now as then, and may be seen danced any night among African hills and valleys if the moon is full.

The people of all the tribes are inheritors of a system of common law, which is admirably adapted to the circumstances in which they live. It has, like their dancing steps, come down to them from a period so remote that its origin is lost in the mists of antiquity. Not only its salient points, but its minutest details, have been transmitted from generation to generation by men who make it their business to master it. All trials are in open court. There is perfect freedom of speech, and as any one can interfere, departure from custom is all but impossible.

This common law is well adapted to people in a rude state of society. It holds every one accused of crime guilty unless he can prove himself innocent; it makes the head of the family responsible for the conduct of all its branches; the village collectively for all resident in it, and the clan for each of its villages. There is no such thing under it as a man professing to know nothing of his neighbour's doings. The law requires him to make himself acquainted with everything in his neighbourhood as a duty which he owes to the community. This doubtless gives rise to injustice occasionally, and especially in the case of persons accused of witchcraft, for which crime the law allows torture to force a confession, and the punishment is death. There are other rare cases in which capital punishment follows conviction.

For the administration of the law there are courts of various grades, from any of which an appeal may be taken to the supreme tribunal council presided over by the paramount chief. The chief can also hear any cause, however trifling, without its passing through any other court. Every member of the tribe has free access to him at all times. He is not only the ruler and military despot, he is also the "father of the people."

Africans measure time by days, moons, and years. The time of day is told by the position of the sun. At night they reckon by the position of well-known stars, and can come wonderfully near the time as reckoned by other means. The month, which consists of the days during which the moon is visible, is reckoned by her phases. The days of darkness between the old and new moon are not counted; the moon has wasted away. The new moon is a true new moon and no reappearance of a worn out orb.

The beginning of the new year is determined by the budding of certain trees and shrubs, after which spring operations commence. They calculate only twelve lunar months for the year, for which they have descriptive names, and this results in frequent confusion and difference of opinion as to which month it really is. The confusion is always rectified by the first appearance of Pleiades just before sunrise, and a fresh start is made and things go on smoothly till once more the moons get out of place, and reference has again to be made to the stars.

The sombre life of an African is relieved occasionally by amusements of which the following are among the most common, war dances always excepted.

Dedera, or cattle running, may be regarded as the national amusement. The cattle are trained for the game, and a race causes as much excitement as turf events do among ourselves. The cattle are taken to a distance from home, and when all is ready, young men running and shouting alongside of them start them off at a run. Presently they break into a clumsy gallop, and this is kept up for miles, all the young men following at top speed. The owner of the successful beast receives the victor's garland. This training to run to a certain cry proves of great value in time of war, as the cattle can be run to a place of safety with little trouble when there is occasion for flight.

Ukumbama (Wrestling).—Two men sit down with crossed legs and grasp each other firmly round the waist. First one and then the other tries to free himself, and they move and roll about more like pigs in a sack than men wrestling. The victor has a feather placed in his hair by the umpire.

Tshotsha.—In this game a number of young men collect and sides are taken, each leader calling out men alternately. One party then goes to a hut where a number of girls are assembled, with a *dikasi*—a woman of easy virtue—on either side of the door.

On entering they give their scanty goat skin garments to the girls to hold, and form a circle kneeling. They then go through most violent contortions of body till the perspiration pours off them, and forming a stream runs along the sloping floor. When they are exhausted and can go on no longer they retire. A mark is made at the spot to which this stream of perspiration has reached; the hut is cleaned and aired, and the second party enter to perform the same exercises. The party whose perspiration runs farthest is declared to be victorious. The girls supply the music by clapping their hands, the men making a grunting noise in unison.

Mention has frequently been made of magicians and witchcraft, and as the whole life of the people is greatly influenced by superstitious fears regarding magic and divination, a brief account of those who practise the art may be interesting. Magicians and witch doctors are of both sexes, and the profession is entered by the candidate first feigning sickness and refusing to eat or move, or even to converse with others. A doctor is then sent for, who makes a careful examination of the patient. If it appears that he is suffering from delusions or any form of mental hallucination, steps are taken for his recovery if possible. If, on the other hand, the doctors conclude that he is preparing for the office of magician, they declare that he is inspired by the spirits, and that he must be left alone. He thereupon adopts singular and peculiar habits, abstains from certain articles of food, professes to have dreams and see visions, and presently becomes a full-fledged doctor, with practically unlimited power over men's lives and property. These men are supposed to effect cures, and as disease and disaster are caused by wizards and witches, the discovery of the criminal is a more important function than the administration of drugs.

When anyone, say a man in middle life, is ill, and the treatment by ordinary means fails, his friends go to the witch doctor's kraal, and sit down, close to it, in a waiting attitude. By-and-by the great man appears, and sitting down at a little distance from the visitors, takes a pinch of snuff. If the visitors ask for tobacco he knows it is but a casual call and enters into ordinary conversation. If they do not ask, he, scenting a case, goes into the house and brings out a dry hide and some sticks. These he throws down before his visitors and says, "You have come about a child." And they, beating softly on the hide with the sticks, reply in a low voice, "We agree." The doctor proceeds, "You have come about a woman." The gentle beating is continued, and the same reply is made as before. The next remark is, "The man you have come about is very ill." They, beating loudly, reply as before, twice repeated. On such lines our friend proceeds till he has learned all he wishes to know about the man, his family circumstances and history. After this he sits in silence for a long while and then says, oracularly, "You are being killed." When asked how and by whom, he replies that he cannot tell; they must return on the morrow—bringing a beast of course—and perhaps the spirits will in the interval reveal to him the author of the evil. The deputation then retire, and when they go home give a neighbour a hint as to whom they suspect, fixing on some one who has a grudge against the patient. This friendly neighbour goes at dead of night and tells the doctor, who is now in a position to act. The next day the beast is driven to his house, and the sick man's friends, having warned the chief of what is going on, proceed to the appointed place fully armed. Attendance on the part of all the neighbours is compulsory. The accused thus marches, in ignorance of his doom, with the cavalcade. On the way he may be asked, casually, "What does the person bewitching our brother deserve?" and he promptly replies, "He must die."

On arrival they find the doctor's men armed—doctors rank as chiefs and are allowed to have armed retainers. The visitors give up their weapons to the men of the village, and the whole party seat themselves in a semi-circle, the chief presiding. From this point the custom varies among different tribes, With some the doctor communicates the accused's name to the chief, who in his turn tells his war minister, and the man is dispatched in his bed that same night. Among others, while a song is being sung, the doctor rushes suddenly up to the doomed man and shouts, "This is the wizard who is bewitching so-and-so." He then runs in among his armed followers, and all the people jump up leaving the culprit sitting alone. He must not move nor may anyone go near him. One of his friends will ask where he got the bewitching medicine, and the doctor, from the safe shelter of his friends' spears, replies, "He bought it at such a place for so many cattle." No one is allowed to plead the cause of the culprit. His friends are disarmed and cannot strike a blow for him if they would, and the poor wretch, utterly confused and confounded, and unwilling to die alone, as often as not accuses some one else of assisting him—denial is utterly useless—and this man also is at once isolated, but he has the right of ordinary trial and may be acquitted. The chief may refuse to have the man executed, in which case he is allowed to leave the territory with bare life. If the sentence is to be carried out he is murdered at a short distance from the doctor's on his way home. It sometimes happens that when the prisoner is ordered to leave, he is able to show a clean pair of heels, in which case he is of course safe on crossing the border.

Rain doctors are a shrewd, clever class of men, who are careful and accurate observers of all indications of change of weather and signs of coming rain. They are generally able to tell with a considerable degree of accuracy when rain is likely to fall, and some of them maintain their reputation unimpaired for many years. If spring rains are later than usual a black ox is sent to the doctor, who, being warned of the approaching deputation, sits in his hut covered with mud, with which he smears himself instead of the ordinary everyday fat. If there are no indications of rain he may either direct them to come again, or order a meeting of the tribe. There is then much eating, drinking, and dancing. Charms are produced and mystic ceremonies performed, and a day is named before which rain is to fall. Should this prediction prove correct, the doctor is liberally rewarded, but if it should not, he must explain his failure. This is always accounted for by some one in high authority working against him; when pressed he may name the chief wife of the paramount chief, or his mother. As these, under African native law, cannot be put to death, the rain-maker cannot bring rain, and is either excused or condemned, according to the humour the chief happens to be in at the time. Chiefs have been known to sacrifice every doctor belonging to the tribe, in one huge holocaust.

If too much rain falls, the doctor, accompanied by a large crowd, repairs to the house of a family where there has been no death for a very long time, and then burns the skin of a coney. He shouts, as it burns, "The rabbit is burning." This cry is taken up, and the whole crowd continue to shout till exhausted. If this does not stop the rain, it is given up as a hopeless case, and they sit down with such resignation as they can, till Nature herself brings relief. When rain falls after the doctor has performed the prescribed ceremonies, there must be no ploughing till his fees are paid.

The class of doctors who protect persons and property from the thunderbolt, have a very safe and lucrative calling. It is seldom lightning strikes twice in succession in the same spot, and after a spot is "doctored," it is almost impossible to detect the imposture. When a man is killed by lightning, nothing can be done till the doctor comes. He removes the dead, sprinkles place and people with medicine. Cattle are then killed in sacrifice, and eaten by the company. Till this last ceremony is performed, all who dwell in the village are unclean. They cannot visit their neighbours, nor can the neighbours come near them. The relatives of the dead must show no signs of mourning. It is said, " Heaven has taken its own," and mourning would be to protest, and might bring punishment. Heaven, in this sense, means the " Dweller in heaven ;" or, in other words, " The great spirit of whom nothing is known." If a tree is struck by lightning, it is dug up by the roots and burned. Thunder is caused by a large mythical bird clapping its wings. Lightning is this bird's excrement, and when lightning strikes any object, the bird has descended to lay its eggs, and ascends again in an invisible mist. If the eggs are not destroyed by the doctors, more lightning birds would be hatched. The eggs are, of course, invisible.

It is the magician's province, among other mystic duties, to foretell events, detect thieves, and discover stolen property; to attend to anything which is new and strange, and explain its meaning. Anything unusual is an excuse for calling in his aid. Domestic animals indulging in gambols of an unusual kind, must be explained. An osprey flying over an army, is waiting for the eyes of the slain, and bodes defeat. The Abyssinian hornbill alighting on a house foretells calamity or death. A frog in a sleeping apartment is a sure sign of bad luck. For these, and many other such causes of death and disaster, the magician is in constant demand, and only through his prompt attendance can the predicted evils be avoided. In this way, the whole domestic life of the African comes to be lived in a constant state of anxiety and fear. He clings to ancient customs, while these gall him like a fetter. Phantoms haunt him in his revelry, and the dark shadows of disaster or death dog his steps on the field of battle, or while tending his flocks amid the silence of his native hills and valleys.

Although the natives of Africa are spirit-worshippers, their doctrine of souls is hazy in the extreme. All human beings have souls, but these are, at times, spoken of as residing in the body; at other times, as having their abode in the roof of a man's house, and changing whenever there is a change of residence. The soul is a separate existence, and, whether residing in the body or house top, has no direct connection with the body, and is not changed by death. When a man dies, his soul leaves by the mouth, and is, for ever afterwards, in attendance upon his descendants. It is, beyond question, this belief in attendant spirits, who always hover about a man's dwelling, which has given rise to the confusion regarding the soul's place of residence before death, and the doubt as to whether it is, or is not, always associated with the body and inseparably joined to it. They have no notion of the condition of the soul, after death, being affected by what life a man lives in the world, and though fully alive to the evils of theft, falsehood, arson, murder, disputings, etc., they have no doctrine of sin, nor any conception of a man's own soul being influenced by his actions, while the souls or spirits of the ancestors are influenced by the most trivial deeds of their descendants. Any departure from custom raises their ire, and they punish their children for their temerity. Devotion to traditional usage brings joy to those who have gone from among men, and they bring health and happiness to the obedient. If a man dies without speaking to his children, while on his death-bed, his soul attends upon them only for purposes of evil, and in such cases all disaster is attributed to this malign influence. Sacrifices are offered to this offended and wandering spirit to prevent misfortune. In certain cases of sickness, the doctor will say that it is caused by the souls of departed relatives who are hungry. A beast is killed to appease them. The flesh is placed in a hut for a whole night, and the spirits feast upon it, drawing out of it the essence on which they feed. Next day, the whole is cooked and eaten, the bones only, and small portions of fat, being burned by the priest, who, at the same time, utters incantations and prayers.

In dreaming, a man's soul passes out of his nostrils, but returns before he is fully awake again. If any one sees a deceased relative in his dreams, he consults a magician, who says the spirit is hungry, and a beast is slain and treated as above related, to appease his appetite. Africans never speak of a man as having died, or being dead. The phrase is, "He is not here," or, "He is no more." There is no transmigration of souls, but the bodies of the dead are, at times, supposed to take the form of the *Tukwakwa*—a deadly species of snake—which the people never kill, for fear of offending the spirits of their ancestors. Departed spirits cannot be driven away nor caught; in fact, no one dare interfere with them in any way, except to honour them by offerings and sacrifice. When a man has had a narrow escape from death, he says, "The soul of my father saved me," and on his return home, if on a journey, he will sacrifice a beast as a thank-offering to his guardian spirit. There are certain streams in which spirits reside, and women on fording these, never raise their clothes, as this would offend them. When there is war, a beast is sacrificed and thrown into the stream. The sacrifice is, however, more to the dead chief as a propitiatory offering for victory, than to those spirits which inhabit the stream. This superstition, though akin to, is different from that regarding river demons, of which there are many, and all of them malign.

There is no resurrection of the dead. When a man "goes away" he shall "never see the sun again," but witch doctors can raise the bodies of the dead, not to reappear again among men, nor possessed of their senses. These raised bodies wander for ever in forests and live in caves. No one ever sees them except magicians. It is for this reason that the graves of chiefs are guarded night and day for years, and that, in many parts, it is customary to bury the dead at night, so that evil persons may not know the grave.

Animals have no souls, but they have a language, only no one has been able to understand it. Domestic cattle, however, do understand our language, and owners of cattle and horses often address them as if they understood every word, and I have at times fancied they do. I have heard a man praise his horse, and the animal walking up to him showing every sign of pleasure. On being told he was an "ugly, lazy, useless brute that ate his corn and did nothing for it," the poor beast walked away as if quite hurt and offended.

Rivers are inhabited by demons or malignant spirits, and it is necessary to propitiate these on crossing an unknown stream, by throwing a handful of corn or some other offering, even if it is of no intrinsic value, into the water. Of these spirits, the *Incanti* corresponds to the Greek Python, while the *Hili* has the appearance of a very small and ugly old man, and is very malevolent. These spirits are never seen except by magicians. To an ordinary person it is certain death to see an *incanti*. When any one is drowned, the magicians say, "He was called by the spirits," and this call no one can resist, nor is it safe to interfere in order to save one who is "called" from drowning. After a death by drowning, the doctors prescribe a formal sacrifice to be offered, but the animal is not killed; it is simply driven into the water, and this is deemed sufficient, or it may happen that the form prescribed shall only include the casting of a few handfuls of corn into the water at the spot where the accident happened. At other times the magicians direct the people to assemble at the river and pelt the spirit with stones, and this is done with great good will, every man and woman shouting the most abusive epithets at the demon. This can only be done when a magician is present to avert evil consequences.

A few years ago, some girls were bathing in the Bashee. One of them got beyond her depth, and the others raised an alarm. Two men working close by came to the river bank but did nothing to save her; it was a clear case of being "called." The British Resident, Mr. Bell, came to hear of it, and summoned the whole party to appear before him. The men acknowledged the facts, and said the water could not be more than breast deep, but, in the circumstances they could not interfere. The magistrates tried to reason with them, but in vain, and at last concluded that "six months hard" might do more to eradicate superstition than all his philosophy, and "six months hard" it accordingly was.

Another case of drowning happened near the Mbulu mission-station. The body lodged under a bank and could not be recovered by ordinary means. The people then drove an ox to the bank, and their magician began praying to the demons to give up the dead, saying, "We offer you sacrifice. It is not the dead we bring; it is blood." But, like Baal of old, "There was no voice, nor any that answered." When they had wearied themselves, the Rev. J. Davidson came to them and proposed to dive and recover the body. To this they vehemently objected on the ground that he would be himself "called." He, however, went into the pool and, to their intense amazement, brought the body to the bank with little trouble. He was, for the time being, regarded as a most powerful magician.

One other illustration I shall give. On a sultry summer's afternoon, I arrived at the Tsitsa, hot and wearied after a long ride, and proposed to have a swim in its clear cool water. I directed my groom to turn the horses loose to graze while I bathed. To my surprise he remonstrated on the ground that there were poisonous water snakes in the Tsitsa. I told him that was nonsense, as water snakes did not bite. This he could not deny generally, but the snakes of the Tsitsa differed from others. I then called him a woman or some other contemptuous name, and told him to do as he was bid. Seeing I was determined, he said, with the greatest awe and solemnity, "The truth is, master, there is a *Tikoloshe* in that pool, and, if you go in, you will be called." I had my swim, my man watching me in terror, but if that *tikoloshe* had been at home, these lines would not have been written, for, according to my faithful black, I should have been certainly "called."

I may here refer to another superstition regarding spirits other than those of their ancestors. At long intervals, beside the great foot-paths of the country, there are large cairns of small stones. All who pass them cast a stone on the cairn. They then give the royal salute, and add, "*Ah! sivivane*" (*i.e.*, hail cairn), "grant us strength and prosperity." On being questioned as to the origin and meaning of these *sivivane*, they profess utter ignorance, and say the prayer is to the great spirit. Another custom observed, in order to secure good fortune in travelling, is to place stones in the forks of trees at the road side, or in grassy country devoid of timber, to knot tufts of grass at intervals. No particular reason is assigned for either custom. It is lucky to do so; that is all.

There are no human sacrifices offered by South African natives, nor have I found very distinct traces of fetish. The nearest approach to it I have observed is a custom in regard to the skull and horns of the animal sacrificed in case of death by lightning. These are placed in the roof of the hut, and must not be touched by any human hand, except by the magician. There they remain for years as an object of veneration and quasi-worship. There are a few animals sacred, as the snake already referred to, the buzzard, certain species of eagle, and a number of other animals, and these are never killed under any circumstances.

A man in hiding chews the leaves of the *umfingwane* to defy detection. Cut finger nails and hair must be buried for fear wizards might get hold of them to work evil. A man must not spit when an enemy is near, as he might get hold of the saliva and give it to a witch-doctor who could use it to his hurt. A woman in time of war places her sleeping mat across the open door; according as the shadow falls her husband is alive and well or dead. At the close of the year all the men procure a violent emetic, which they swallow. From March to October young girls must not take milk, as the cows are then troubled with ticks. Medicines can be had from witch-doctors to secure the favour of women; to ensure safety when on predatory expeditions; to ruin a rival, and even to cause the death of an enemy. These are, however, not got from the recognised doctors, but rather from those who practise the illegal arts of necromancy and witchcraft.

At the beginning of the year the whole tribe repair to the "great place," where the doctors rub a powder into a small incision made in the forehead. Stepping over a person sleeping is highly improper, and if a wife steps over her husband he cannot hit his enemy in war; if over his assegais they are from that time useless, and are given to boys to play with, so too with his walking sticks. Green wood must not be cut while the crops are growing, as blight or hail would follow. If the extremity of a rainbow rests upon a stream or pool of water, people will not bathe at that spot, nor are the girls allowed to fetch water from it while the rainbow is supposed to be there. Should they go they would find a huge bason with an *incanti*, "which would swallow them up in a heap." High winds are caused by malevolent wizards and warlocks. Earthquakes portend frightful wars, while eclipses are the harbingers of evils that cannot be known.

The African's notions of creation and the origin of death are very hazy, but all the same he has a theory regarding the latter at least; and some crude notions of the former also. It is supposed that the never-dying *Sudiwa* made man, and placed him in a certain spot. One day the Sudiwa sent *Unwaba*—the chameleon—with a message to say that men were to live for ever. The *Untulo*—a species of lizard—overheard the message given to Unwaba, and being anxious to appear of importance, and also having a grudge against the Unwaba, set out immediately, and, being swift of foot, arrived while the Unwaba was still struggling in the marshes. He then said that the never-dying Sudiwa had sent him to say that people were to die, and after that he returned again before the true messenger arrived. When the Unwaba arrived with his important communication the people said to him, "Go, false one, we have already heard the words of the never-dying Sudiwa from the Untulo, and many people have perished." Thus death came into the world by a fraud.

Among the virtues of the tribes of Southern Africa, fidelity to their chiefs must be reckoned first. For his chief a man will lie and steal, commit the meanest of actions and submit to every form of indignity, and the more a man is called upon to do and to suffer the higher his virtue. In ordinary life one does not expect to find truth a prominent virtue among savages, but if a Bantu undertakes the charge of any form of property, he accounts for it with as great fidelity as if he were the Keeper of the Great Seal. But, on the other hand, there are many circumstances in which falsehood is not reckoned even a disgrace, and if a man could extricate himself from difficulties by lying and did not do so, he would be simply thought a fool. The deceptive power of the average African is something wonderful to Europeans; he can lie without a change of countenance or the movement of a muscle, though he knows that conviction is a certainty, nor does he greatly concern himself when falsehood is clearly brought home to him; he simply regards his defence as having failed.

Another prominent virtue is hospitality. To so great an extent is this carried that food becomes almost common property. Any one passing by a village at meal time, friend or stranger, provided only he is not inferior in rank, sits down without invitation or ceremony and shares in the meal. Most villages have a hut set apart specially for the use of strangers, and all these courtesies are extended to Europeans as well as to natives.

Among the mountain tribes, there are ceremonies by which the youths are formed into guilds or lodges with passwords. The members of these lodges are bound never to give evidence against one another. The rites of initiation are peculiar, and deserving of notice. One of them is that of infusing courage, intelligence, and other qualities. Whenever an enemy who has acted bravely is killed, his liver, which is considered the seat of valour, his ears which are the seat of intelligence, the skin of his forehead from which he gets his perseverance, and other members, each of which is considered to be the seat of some virtue, are cut from his body, and baked to cinders. The ashes are carefully preserved in the horn of a bull, and, during the circumcision ceremonies, are mixed with other ingredients into a kind of paste, and administered by the tribal priest to the youths. The idea being that the virtues which they represent are communicated to those who swallow them. This along with the removal of parts of the bodies of the slain by the war doctor for his medicines, accounts for the frequent mutilation of bodies, rather than any inherent barbarity in prosecuting war. Certain tribes deem it necessary to make a large incision in the abdomen of the slain, to prevent gas being generated which magicians could use to their hurt.

In married life, among the coast tribes, chastity

can hardly be said to exist. By custom every wife of a polygamist has a lover, and no woman sinks in the esteem of her companions on this being known. Favoured guests among the hill men have female companions allotted to them, and the chief often secures the services and adherence of young men, too poor to purchase wives, by temporarily or permanently bestowing one of his own concubines on them. Still virtue has a value, as is seen by the care with which the harems of a few of the more powerful chiefs are guarded. It might be thought that society would fall to pieces if life were more immoral than this, and yet the domestic life at the kraal of a mountain chief is even more vile. A description is, of course, impossible.

There is a curious theory current among a number of South African tribes regarding their own origin as separate peoples. Universal tradition points to the north as their original home, but how they wandered away from it is seldom explained, and many profess entire ignorance of the causes which lead to a change of country and home. The tradition referred to accounts for the migration as follows :—The great chief whose people occupied the whole of the centre of Africa, and whose name was Uhlanga, had a law forbidding women to marry before a certain age on pain of direst punishment.

Long ago, "so long that all memory of their exploits is lost," Uhlanga sent a great army, the greatest ever mustered at one time, on an expedition towards the south. This army, which was to be absent a long time, and was to conquer all peoples to the farthest sea, was accompanied by numbers of young women as cooks. After an absence of three years, during which the army met and destroyed a very great number of tribes, the waves of the sea stopped its advance. The soldiers then gave themselves up to rest and enjoyment, and only after they had grown fat eating captured cattle, did they think of their homes and their children. After the march northwards was continued many days, it was found that all the girl cooks were *enceinte*. This caused consternation and terror among all ranks, and for fear of punishment and death the whole army retraced its steps towards the south, and arrived in the country of the Bushmen. There the generals divided the companies between them, and settled down to the pursuit of agriculture. They never had any tidings of their wives or children, nor did any of them return to their old home. Uhlanga thought that his army had perished, and never again sent an expedition to that country.

The resemblance of this tradition to the well-known classical story is so close as to make one at first doubt its originality, but it is found among those peoples who have had least contact with Europeans, from whom alone they could learn the legends of the days when Rome was young. To account for the origin of such traditions is extremely difficult. That many of the tribes of the south came from the north is proved beyond all doubt by the affinity of language, and the substantial identity of customs and habits. When we endeavour to account for the various types met with, and the vast differences, physical and otherwise, between them, we find it impossible to refer to a common origin such widely differing peoples as Bushmen, Hottentots, and Zulus. The first seem to have, as it were, fallen out of their proper place among the family of African nations, and seem more akin to the aborigines of Australia.

When questioned regarding distances, and the time it would take to travel " to their home," in connection with such traditions as the above, the African's ideas are altogether haze. He has no conception of the extent of his own continent. He understands nothing of lands beyond the sea. The Englishman came " out of the sea in his ships." If a man travels east or west, he never could return from the opposite direction, even if he could walk over the sea. At some place he would come to the end of the world, and there would be nothing to prevent his falling down ; and if he could get underneath the world, how could he walk round, " like a fly, with his feet above his head, to return from the other side." There are no people on the lower side of the world, and if men could dig a hole deep enough it would go through, and one falling into it would " fall away into empty space below."

The sun goes round underneath, and comes up again out of a great hole. " The white man is foolish when he says the sun does not move, for do we not see the movement as he rises and sets; and how could he be on the east in the morning, and on the west at night if he stood still." As to the earth revolving, how can that be, "Is man a fly that he could walk with his body hanging down when the world turned."

The sun is a great ball of fire. Man himself found out how to make fire. No one taught him, but the way to produce it has been always known. There are curious legends and customs connected with the production of fire, and that not only in Africa, but among almost all peoples. The Celtic clans had an ancient observance, of which traces remained till within the last hundred years. At a given time all fires were extinguished, and then men produced new fire by friction. From this *Teine eigin*, as it was called, all the neighbouring families obtained fire brands with which to kindle their domestic fires. This was observed as an annual custom, the neglect of which brought misfortune.

When the native Africans use special fire, either in connection with sacrifice or the festival of first-fruits, it is produced by a doctor, and in the following manner:—Two sticks, made of the *Uzwati* tree, and called the "husband and wife," are given to him by the chief. These sticks are prepared by the magicians, and are the exclusive property of the chief, the "wife" being the shorter of the two. The doctor cuts a piece off each stick, and proceeds to kindle fire in the usual manner, by revolving the one rapidly between the palms of his hands, while its end rests in a small hollow dug in the side of the other. After he has obtained fire, he gives it to his attendant, who gets the pots in order, and everything ready for cooking the newly-reaped fruits. The sticks are handed back to the chief by the doctor—no other hand must touch them—and put away till they are required next season. They are regarded as in a measure sacred, and no one, except the chief's personal servant, may go to the side of the hut where they are kept. After being repeatedly used for fire-making, the doctor disposes of what remains, and new ones are made and consecrated by the magician.

A special pot is used for the preparation of the feast, and no other than it may be set on a fire produced from the "husband and wife." When the feast is over, the fire is carefully extinguished, and the pot placed along with the sticks, where it remains untouched for another year.

It is highly improper to kindle a fire in certain circumstances. There is a legend that when Unsha arrived in what is now Natal, having been preceded by a division of his army under his eldest son, he saw smoke rising as from a newly kindled fire. He sent to inquire whose doing it was, and, on being told his son had kindled it, he sent for him and addressed him thus:—" From this day you are no longer heir to the chieftainship of my people. Your first act on entering the enemy's country was to make a fire.

That shows you will destroy my people." His second son was appointed heir, and he in turn offended his father by giving an order, the result of a foolish whim, that the first milk from every cow that calved was to be brought to him. The verdict in his case was :—"You rob the calves. When you are old you will suck blood." The third son was appointed heir, and became his father's successor.

Offended spirits often show their displeasure by causing some form of illness to attack either the person who has offended them or one of his family. When the magicians are called, if they decide that the malady is the work of spirits, they order a beast to be killed, and this is eaten, but should the sick person die in the interval between the order and the eating of the flesh, the whole is thrown to the dogs. It may not be touched by men.

In certain cases of illness, and before magician or witch-doctor is consulted, a relative of the sick person will take his stand at the door and call upon his ancestors to say what is the cause of this trouble. All the cattle belonging to the village are then driven to the door, and the first that makes water gets a deep prod from an assegai. If the animal bellows, it is the one selected by the spirits, and it is slaughtered and treated in the following manner :—A gash is made in its side, and into this a man inserts his hand. He then seizes hold of the abdominal aorta which he tears away and breaks. He next extracts as much fat as he can remove with his fingers, and this is immediately burned on a fire already prepared in the sick man's house. The beast is then cleaned, and the right fore quarter carried into the hut, a piece of which is broiled and given to the patient. The remainder of the beast is eaten; the bones being burned as sacrifice. Animals slaughtered at certain tribal gatherings have the front leg and shoulder sliced off, and are then allowed to limp about till they bleed to death. The shoulder removed is cut to pieces and roasted on strong fires previously prepared, and is often eaten, and the bones burning among the embers before the victim is quite dead. The cruelties practised on animals prepare us to hear of barbarities practised on men where torture is resorted to, but this is a subject which, in these pages, it is perhaps best to avoid.

When a man has been slain in war, the doctor visits the village and prepares medicine which he mixes with fat and small chips of an exceedingly bitter tree—sneezewood. This he sets on fire in his hands, and blows the smoke over the relatives and assembled friends. The smoke drives away the assegai from them, and no further calamity happens.

When a married woman dies, the husband eats bitter herbs, and goes out for several days tending the cattle, returning home after dark. When a husband dies, the widow goes away from home, and remains on the open plain or mountain for ten days and nights irrespective of the condition of the weather. If he falls in battle, she does not go out, but must remain in her hut and neither clean it nor herself for ten days.

Among the mountain tribes of Basutoland there is a curious custom regarding an enemy who falls after displaying conspicuous courage :—They immediately cut out his heart and eat it, as this is supposed to give them his courage and strength in battle. Other portions, as mentioned elsewhere, are used by war-doctors and magicians for their arts. The man who slays such an enemy is, at the close of the war, called before the chief and gets from the doctor a medicine which he chews with his food. The third day after this he must wash, and, at the expiry of ten days, may return to his wives and children.

Turning from war and its usages to the daily life of the African, we find that the apparently easy and aimless existence of the Kaffir village is one of elaborate ritual and rigid adherence to forms. The staple food of an African consists of grain, milk, and the flesh of animals. The latter is only eaten at feasts, and among animals that are unclean to men, though not in all cases to women, are all birds of prey, animals with uncloven hoofs, monkeys, and many others. On the other hand, women may not eat ox tongue, and the flesh of bulls is, in certain cases, forbidden to them.

A newly made bride may not eat the flesh from the ribs of any animal, and, under certain conditions, married women may not eat flesh from the fore leg. Women wear the knuckle bones of the right front leg round their wrists as a charm. Milk is forbidden to women at periodical intervals, and should they at such time taste it, the cattle would die. Portions of the entrails may not be eaten by men under any circumstances. The lungs, neck, and breast parts are eaten by boys only. Women must never eat the breast parts. Beasts killed by doctors in case of sickness are not touched by women till cooked and ready for use. A woman must not enter the cattle fold, and she must approach and leave her hut by certain paths and not by others. When several brothers have their food together, the elder presides at the pot, and, when the others lift a portion, they praise him and recount his virtues. If they neglect this, they are severely reprimanded, and may be punished by the father. The head of the household never quite finishes what he has on his plate, and the eldest son is the only one who is allowed to take what is left and lick the plate.

At public entertainments, if a man of inferior rank is appointed by the host to wait upon guests of tribal standing they will not accept food at his hands. The usual customs at large gatherings is, to appoint one from among the guests to act as master of ceremonies as regards his tribe's men. I once got into a curious difficulty through neglect of the correct etiquette. At a church opening at Somerville about a thousand persons were present, representing six or eight distinct tribes. A man was appointed to wait on a party of Pondomise whom they regarded as not only of inferior rank, but an upstart from another tribe who wished to be recognised as a subordinate chief. Not a man would taste the food provided, and only after profuse apologies and explanations tendered in the most public manner could their wrath be appeased. The error was excused on the ground of my "ignorance of custom," and after that, good fat beef did the rest, and all dispersed in great good humour.

If a stranger enters a hut and spits, he is guilty of the direst offence a man can commit. He may be spitting bewitching medicine with his saliva, and may deem himself lucky if he leaves with whole bones. Should he be seen lifting cow dung or stray hairs from the cattle's tails he is in no better case than if found expectorating, while placing anything about the cattle-fold or the thatch of the hut, if only a bit of wood or grass, is conclusive proof of evil designs, and from that day forward he is a marked man.

These and a hundred other ceremonies and usages are daily observed. They enter into the domestic life of the people, and any departure from them is regarded as a sign of mental aberration, and the unfortunate individual is by the whole community treated as a lunatic. Men who through sheer force of character rise above small superstitious usages are rare, and when we do meet with such, the universal suspicion with which they are regarded makes them almost doubt their own sanity, and whether it is not really true that is asserted by all men with the sanction of perhaps twenty generations of tradition. They are to be pitied rather than envied, and only when they are brought into contact with European thought and civilisation do their faculties find a field for their exercise, and their talent asserts itself in such works as the translation of the Pilgrim's Progress by Soga, which is a marvel of accuracy and lucidity of expression.

There is among the Bacas a curious custom in connection with courtship and marriage. A young man first tells some of his friends that he admires a certain girl, and after a stated period he speaks to her and says he would like to *twala*, *i.e.*, carry her off. If she is agreeable to this *twala* she mentions a day, and he then carries her off by stealth to his parents' village. Whether his parents like it or not they cannot possibly, under the sanction of custom, refuse to receive her, and she remains at their village for three days under their care and guardianship. On the third day she is returned to her father's house with the dowry cattle. If he accepts the cattle the marriage is arranged to take place at an early date, and her lover does not see her again till the ceremonies are over. Should the girl's father refuse the cattle and return them, the affair takes end. The young people are not in any way consulted regarding their feelings in the matter, nor does it ever occur to an African that this should be done under any circumstances.

In the matter of personal adornment the African has not a large choice, but he makes the most of what he has. Skins of goats, sheep, antelopes, and domestic cattle go to the manufacture of everyday attire. Robes of office, and bridal robes for the great wife of a paramount chief on the occasion of her marriage are of more costly material, generally of wild cat or spotted leopard skin, the latter being regarded as the most valuable.

The men of the Pondomise tribes have an extraordinary method of dressing their hair. The framework of the head dress is formed by placing a small ring of grass on the crown of the head. The hair is then rubbed well into the grass with fat, and securely sewn with thread made from the sinews of an ox. It is then greased and dressed every day, and the circlet rises with the growth of the hair till it attains an elevation of several inches above the head. It is never removed till colonies are formed under shelter of its dense mass, and when these become numerous the man whose head-gear was the pride of of his life appears with clean shaven pate.

The hair is often adorned with feathers, tufts of rat or monkey skin, and the fantasies of magicians. The most extraordinary head-dress I ever saw was composed of blown bladders in the form of a coronet. The wearer, a royal messenger, had been on a long journey, and, according to custom, was presented with the bladders of all animals killed in his honour. On his return home he manufactured them into the most original head-dress ever devised by mortal man, and stalked about carrying with him at once the evidence of the honour with which he was received on his travels and his own ingenuity.

To the European who studies native manners, nothing is more marvellous than the power exercised by the magicians, and the implicit obedience that is given to them by all classes of the community from the chief downwards. Their predictions may fail, thieves may go unpunished, rain may not fall, patients may die, but the magicians remain a sacred order, and every failure is explained away, and the fetters of superstition remain unbroken. "The ancestors paid reverence to the magicians; they are angry when their children depart from their customs, and punish them. If we disregard the voice of the ancestors, as it comes to us by the mouth of those who have communication with the spirit world, evil shall befall us." This is the beginning and end of argument, and men, who have for years been in contact with Europeans, practise all that is ordained by custom, with the same fidelity as is done by those who never heard of any system other than their own.

There are others again who value the whole genus of magicians at their true worth, and who from motives of policy rather than faith, observe the ancient customs. Such was my old neighbour, the Gcaleka chief, Segidi. A conservative beyond most in all matters of traditional usages, he was fully alive to more modern methods of conducting his business. While his war-doctor was in a trance waiting for communications from the spirit world regarding the success of an expedition, Segidi's spies travelled the whole length of the enemy's country, and brought him back an accurate report of the probable strength of the opposing force and their tactics in the field. Again, while liberally rewarding his tribal priests and doctors for warding off evil and upholding the traditions, he came to me with three of his sons to send them to school at Blythswood, where they remained for years, to return carrying with them that which never can be assimilated with the old life, be they professed Christians or heathens.

There are times when the shrewdest of magicians are baffled. At a head-man's near us, something had gone wrong. I do not remember what, but the magician was called. He ascribed the evil to river demons, and prescribed the sacrifice of a black ox. The animal was to be shut up in a separate fold for forty-eight hours, after which it was to be turned out when it would walk to the spot where the demon resided. The beast was secluded as ordered. A young teacher from Lovedale went at dead of night and gave it a plentiful supply of water. At the appointed hour it was set free, but instead of going to the demon-haunted pool it began to graze, nor would it be driven to the river. Konke in his wrath exclaimed, "Slay the beast," and slain it promptly was. The magician, finding his chief in such evil humour, slipped away, nor did I ever hear of the sacrifice being completed.

My old evangelist Nteto was a curious mixture of

the Christian and the heathen. In his own life much of the old faith and practice remained, but he was none the less severe on other converts who departed by a hair's breadth from mission rules. A few weeks before I left Africa, he came to me to lodge a complaint against a Christian woman for the practice of heathen rites. She had called a magician to treat a child of hers who was ill, and had also had some dealings with a lightning doctor, who had placed a peg in the roof of her house to secure it from the thunderbolt. After a little questioning, I discovered that the child was treated by a medicine man, and told my evangelist that any one could with a good conscience call a black medicine man, just as he would call an ordinary European practitioner. Into the second count of the inditement I did not feel disposed to enter on the eve of my leaving the country, and in order to get rid of my friend, said to him :—

"How do you come to me about this when your own magistrate has been erecting a lightning rod at his office?"

"That is true, but the magistrate's is a large tree, while this was a small peg on which the magician put medicine."

"The size is nothing, if this woman's doctor had the strongest magic, and as for medicine, go to the magistrate's and you can see the medicine; it is a hoop of copper running up its whole length."

The facts could not be denied. Nteto left uncertain whether to understand the missionary's language as in joke or not, but fully convinced there was something wrong with his reasoning, though he could not exactly tell what it was.

Native Africans have great attachment to their children, and bestow great care on their training. The heir of the house is his father's constant companion. From earliest years he is instructed in all the traditions of his house, and the history of his tribe. He is educated in the theory and practice of law, and learns to recite songs commemorative of deeds of valour. Hatred of traditional enemies is instilled into his mind from the first dawn of intelligence, and he grows up with all the feelings of rancour cherished by those who were first wronged by the people he is taught to hate. Duplicity, cunning, and falsehood are among the virtues instilled into his mind by those who have charge of his education.

Bantu tribes have always behaved honourably towards guests and strangers in time of war. If a man enters the territory, whether missionary, trader, or soldier, as the guest of the tribe, he is treated honourably in time of war, and allowed to preserve a strict neutrality. In the case of war between Europeans and Africans, the latter conducted all white men within their territory to the border, and saw them sent safely to their own people. I do not know one instance in which a man who was the guest of the tribe, lost his life, except by accident. Many have lost their lives during war, and that through cold-blooded murder, but these were men who entered the territory on their own responsibility, or under the wing of a foreign power, and not men who resided there as the guests of the chief, and for the time being subject to him.

One can in time of peace travel from tribe to tribe for a thousand miles, with no other weapon than a walking stick, and never be molested. Wherever he goes he meets with hospitality, and shares in meals at the villages he passes. It is only after the slave raider and land grabber have worked their will with the country, that travelling becomes dangerous. Nor need we wonder that men whose parents were shot, and whose brothers and sisters were carried off to market like so many oxen, should be suspicious of strangers, and try to resist their passing through their country.

Taken all in all, Africans are a noble people. Sunk in superstition it is true, but with excellent traits of character showing underneath the incongenial crust. Their life is sombre, and has little to cheer and lighten it. The slaver, war and superstitious fears, are their constant companions, nor have they yet fully realised the blessings, and the power; the peace and the prosperity that is represented by Christian missions on the one hand, and European thought and commerce—that running ulcer the liquor traffic always excepted—on the other.

That they are brave has been demonstrated on a thousand hard-fought fields, and that they can meet death with resignation and courage, when all the excitement of the field of battle is wanting, is shown by their behaviour in cases of shipwreck and other calamities.

A few years ago an explosion took place in one of the Kimberley Diamond mines. The wood-work of the main shaft caught fire. The workings were filled with smoke, and all egress was apparently cut off, while nothing could be done from above ground.

At the time of the accident a large number of men, European and native, were underground. Of the former several who were overpowered by the first rush of smoke, were carried to a place of temporary safety by the natives, who did all in their power to save their companions, though face to face with death themselves. One European, while trying to make his way into some old workings, came across a group of natives, calmly filling their pipes, as if preparing to have a social smoke together, a common custom among them. He remonstrated, and urged them to seek a place of safety. Their reply was, "We have tried every opening; we know the mine well; there is no hope for any one who is here, and we are going to smoke together before we die." No persuasion would induce them to move. He left them there, and with difficulty reached a place of safety. A week later he conducted a search party to a group of bodies which lay in a circle, their pipes still in their hands or lying on the ground close beside them.

As the African is the slave of custom in his public

life, whether political, religious, or ceremonial, so too he adheres to customary usage, with all the devotion of a Fakir, in his private relations. The observances connected with social etiquette are strictly regulated by custom, and must on no account be departed from. The newly arrived traveller gets a bit of fat with which to anoint his weary limbs. He sits in a particular place at meals, and has a servant set apart to wait upon him. If a man of note, a sheep or ox is killed in his honour, and the whole carcass presented to him. He returns the left fore leg to the chief or head-man, and the remainder he keeps for himself and his attendants, inviting the men of the village to share the prepared food with them. All the years I spent in Africa, I never slept at a chief's village without having a whole sheep presented to me. I have, however, in turn, presented a good many to distinguished visitors at the mission.

Then, again, the forms of salutation between man and man, between men and women, and between chief and people, are matters of ceremonial etiquette, from which no departure is permitted, except at the saturnalia following certain festivals. Even in sleeping, there are certain rules to be observed, and a married man must never occupy the right hand side of the bed. Custom regulates a man's habits as regards bathing, washing, smearing himself with fat simply, or with fat and red ochre; the cutting of his hair and trimming of his beard, as well as the articles of food he is to eat at different hours of the day.

From his cradle to his grave he is the slave of ancient usage and superstition. In his life there is nothing free, nothing original, nothing spontaneous, no progress towards a higher and better life, and no attempt to improve his condition, mentally, morally, or spiritually.

Such are some of the social customs practised by the people among whom I lived in Africa. Customs which have the sanction of perhaps a thousand years of tradition, and to which the people are welded with all the attachment of superstitious fears and the veneration paid to their ancestors. Customs from which any departure involves untold woes, and the loss of all sympathy among one's friends and neighbours. To break down this system of superstition, cruelty, and oppression, is the task to which the missionary has to address himself, and in its place to instil the knowledge of One, who long ago came to set men free from all the thraldom of superstition and sin. This, and to introduce into that dark land the ideas of civilised life was the work in which I spent the busiest years of my life, with what success it is not for me or for others to say. Only when the morning breaks, and the shadows flee away, shall it be known what influence any effort has exerted upon individuals and communities, and especially upon peoples slowly emerging from a state of barbarism.

X.

STRAY STUDIES OF ANIMAL LIFE.

DURING my wanderings I made frequent notes of any peculiarities I observed in the habits of animals and insects, and also of the geological formation of the country. The latter is too wide a field to enter upon in these pages; nor could I add much to what has already been written upon the subject. There is, however, one very remarkable geological gap or cleft in the Transkei, the course of which I followed for nearly fifty miles. It extends from the valley of the Kei, which it joins about forty-five miles above its mouth, to the coast, at a point about twenty miles east of the place where the river enters the sea. Its course is almost geometrically straight, and it preserves a uniform depth, irrespective of valleys and hills, except where it has been silted up by soil washed down from the neighbouring heights. Along part of its course it divides basalt and granite formations, and again basalt and gneiss; near the sea the division is between primary rocks and sandstone, and at various points schists crop up through the soil. These rocks are not wholly confined to one side or another, but may be seen on either side of the cleft, though on the main the division is between different rocks. I have sought in vain for glacier action along its sides. I could find no trace of glaciation in any portions of it I examined, and cannot with confidence propound any theory regarding its origin.

Another peculiarity seen near Pirie, is the so-called comijtes or cups. These cups are from three to twelve feet in diameter and about four feet deep, divided by ridges from four to ten feet across. They cover the surface for many miles, and have puzzled geologists to explain their origin and formation. To me they were a hopeless riddle. There seemed to be no force adequate to account for so much surface disturbance, which was plainly recent. The theory of the action of water had to be rejected, as they covered both hill and dale to the very crest. The action of fire was out of the question. Earth-worms might account for it, but why should they work among the ridges and not in the hollows? and why in that locality and not in others in the neighbourhood? Besides, there were no worms in any numbers to be seen there, and that seemed final against them.

Several years after I had tried to account for the Pirie comijtes, and after the subject had quite passed from my mind, I one day noticed the same peculiarity in actual formation. I was riding along a valley in East Griqualand, where the soil was loose and porous, and noticed an extraordinary quantity of soil turned up by earth-worms. It lay on the ground in all directions like small coils of very stout twine, and seemed as if this had been repeated daily for weeks or months. On examining the ground more closely, and going down nearer the bottom of the valley, I found that the worms did not work over the whole surface, and that as I neared the river distinct hollows were formed where the worms did not work; in other words, they were busily engaged in raising ridges. Half-a-mile farther up the valley the ground presented the same appearance as at Pirie, and hardly a trace of the work going on so busily lower down could be seen. The entire colony of earth-worms seemed as if migrating and forming comijtes as they went. The mystery was solved, and indirect but valuable confirmation afforded of Darwin's theory of the action of earth-worms on the surface soil in Europe.

But the action of earth-worms in Africa is very limited, and only where there are peculiar conditions of earth are they met with, or if found, so deep down, following the moisture, as to have hardly any influence on the soil near the surface. But the surface soil needs to be constantly renewed for the nourishment of plants and grasses, and we must look for some other agent who performs the service rendered by earth-worms in temperate latitudes. Nor do we look in vain. In Africa, wherever the soil is dry and hard, the ground is literally studded with ant heaps. These are formed of solid particles of soil, dug laboriously from underneath the ground, and carried to the surface, where they are built into the hard mortar walls that form the nest. I have often sliced away a portion of an ant heap, exposing the tunnelled structure of its interior, and then watched the process of repair, as that is promptly carried on by these active workers of the colony, under superintendence of soldier ants. The building process is as follows:—An ant appears with a particle of earth, held firmly in its mandibles, and when it arrives at the spot where the stone is to be placed, it rolls it round once or twice, covering it over with some gelatinous substance from its own body. It then places it in position, rams it down tightly, and immediately disappears for another load. This process goes on without intermission till the breach is repaired, when the nest assumes its normal appearance. These nests, though very hard and durable, are not imperishable, and thousands of them may be counted in all stages of decay. When a colony abandons its old home and builds a new nest, the old one is gradually worn away by the action of heavy drenching tropical rain and wind. The particles comprising it are spread over the surface of the soil, and restore its exhausted fertility. In this way the ants are constantly engaged bringing new earth to the surface, and carrying on the process of change. The magnitude of the work done can only be realised by those who have seen these enormous heaps so closely huddled together over the African plain. The process is no doubt slow. What the farmer does with his team of horses and sharp ploughshare in a single season nature's ploughmen take years to perform; but still the work is done, and the process of growth and decay goes on with all the regularity of the returning sun.

The habits of ants are so well known as to need no repetition here, but there is one variety which for destructive properties beggars every creature on the face of the earth. I refer to the much abused white ant or termite. The creature, the workers of which are stone blind, lives almost exclusively upon decayed wood, and no sooner is a trunk felled or fallen than they begin operations upon it, and if unchecked reduce tons of sound timber to dust in a few months. Nothing comes amiss to them. The timbers of a house, its floorings, bookshelves, tables, trunks of wood or leather, felt hats, boots, clothes, anything and everything, metal and stone alone excepted, which comes within reach of these marauders is instantly attacked and destroyed. I have seen bullocks' horns, which had lain for some time on the ground, attacked by them and no small progress made in eating them away. The creatures never appear above ground when they can help it; for by night and by day enemies are on the watch for them, and yet they procure most of their food from decayed branches high up in the forest trees. How they manage this, without once appearing above ground, is charmingly told by Professor Drummond in his "Tropical Africa," from which the following quotation is taken. Mr. Drummond says:—

" It is clear the darkness is no protection to the white ant, and yet without coming out of the ground it cannot live. How does it solve the difficulty? It takes the ground out along with it. I have seen white ants working on the top of a high tree, and yet they were under ground. They took up some of the ground with them to the tree top, just as the Esquimaux heap up snow, building it into the low tunnel-huts in which they live; so the white ants collect earth, only in this case not from the surface, but from some depth underneath the ground, and plaster it into tunnelled ways. Occasionally those run along the ground, but more often mount in endless ramifications to the top of trees, meandering along every branch and twig, and here and there debouching into large covered chambers which occupy half the girth of the trunk. . . . The method of building the tunnels and covered ways is as follows : At the foot of the tree the tiniest hole cautiously opens in the ground close to the bark. A small head appears with a grain of earth clasped to its jaws. Against the tree trunk this earth-grain is deposited, and the head is withdrawn. Presently it appears with another grain of earth, this is laid beside the first, rammed tight against it, and again the builder descends underground for more."

While we were at Duff, I had occasion to move a heavy article of furniture, and while so engaged my foot went through the floor. The house was comparatively new, having been built a few years previously, and for a moment I thought there must be a spring under the foundations, and that the timber had decayed; but only for a moment. An examination of the broken board showed the ravages of white ants, the existence of which had not been suspected. I then began to examine the room more closely for traces of their destructive work, and found several tunnels in course of formation. Being anxious to learn something more of their habits than I had had an opportunity of observing, I replaced the broken board and left them to their work. For a week I daily watched their work of tunnel-building and destruction as closely as I could. Their covered ways advanced with marvellous rapidity, and branched out in every direction. Of these branches, several came to an abrupt end, for no sooner did they meet with an obstruction of stone or metal, than the tunnel was closed up and left there as a *cul de sac*. In the building of these tunnels, each worker brought a particle of earth to the top, and after covering it over with slime, placed it with the greatest accuracy in its place, ramming it tight down with its jaws, and then disappeared for more. During all this time a few soldier ants stood on sentry to guard against surprise from other insects, but being inside and comparatively safe, the watch was not kept with the same vigilance as when the tunnel is being carried up the side of a forest tree, nor did the workers observe the same caution in exposing their bodies to view. On removing the book-shelves and flooring—for this process took place in my study—the latter was found to be almost entirely eaten away, and the solid beams underneath were reduced to a shell so thin that one could tear them to pieces with his fingers. An excavation of nearly four feet deep had to be made before the colony was completely removed, and the underground chambers were not the least interesting portion of their home.

In Africa the termites' nest is turned to economic account. It makes the best mortar for house building, where clay mortar is used ; it is free from rough pebbles ; it is tenacious, and it resists the action of rain better than any other form of clay mortar used. It is also largely used by natives for flooring their huts. A floor made of it becomes so hard and smooth, as to be superior to any other substance I have seen used for a similar purpose. It is vastly better than the finest clay worked up by artificial means, and lasts for many years, with no other repair than being occasionally smeared over with cow dung, and then smoothed down with a flat stone. White ant nests in South Africa seldom exceed five feet in height ; in Central Africa, they attain a height of twelve feet or even more. The inhabitants are seldom seen above ground, but this is due to the desire for self-protection, for the moment a white ant appears above the surface, there are a dozen enemies ready to pounce upon it and devour it. Nor does the darkness afford any protection. In Africa, night is the great feeding time, when all the carnivora sally forth to prey upon whatever suits them. Beasts, birds, and insects, are then intent on the great business of life, and the forest, which at noon-time was drowsy and sleepy is now all awake, and its denizens on the alert for attack and defence.

The termites have one enemy whose attack they cannot resist, and that is the ant bear (*Orycteropus Capensis*). This is an animal measuring between three and four feet in length. Its habits are nocturnal and subterraneous, and its food consists of the white ants. It burrows into their nests, and, after disarranging their quarters with its paws, licks them up with its long glutinous tongue. I have seen its burrows four feet deep, and running under the ground for many yards, showing the extent of the excavations made by the termites in building up their heaps above ground.

Though Africa is the home of antelopes I have had very little opportunity of observing their habits closely. In the different frontier districts they are almost extinct, and though on the upland plains I have seen large droves of them, it was generally while travelling in public conveyances and when one could not spend an hour watching them. Once or twice in the forests of East Griqualand, when sitting quietly in the bed of a stream watching the movements of birds and insects, I have seen a few antelopes close at hand, and what was most remarkable about them was the close resemblance between the colours and markings of their skins and the surrounding vegetation. Those whose home is in the forest resemble the undergrowth so closely as to be scarcely distinguishable from the shrub bushes about them till they

R

move, while others, whose home is in the open plain, have exactly the same shade as the grass when browned by the African sun. Their form and motion are extremely graceful, and as they bound over the plain one has hardly the heart to pull a trigger at creatures so inoffensive and so handsome.

African birds have, as a rule, magnificent plumage, but are poor songsters. The Cape Thrush is a sweet singer, but inferior to our own. The Pomerops and so-called Creepers are also songsters, but one feels disappointed after contrasting their modest notes with their splendid plumage. Among the larger birds, the Secretary Bird (*Falco Serpentarius*) is one of the most interesting. Its name—secretary—is derived from a few long feathers which grow behind its head, and hang over its neck and shoulders like a quill behind a scrivener's ear. It is long legged, and resembles in some respects a wader rather than a bird of prey. It inhabits dry open plains, and wanders about all day looking for snakes and lizards on which it feeds. When it discovers a snake it attacks it with the short rudimentary quills at the end of its wings, which are strong and sharp. The mode of attack is peculiar. It runs past the snake with its wing on the ground, and the sharp quills tear the animal's flesh like a hook. After a few such scores across its back the quarry becomes an easy prey. The Secretary, on account of its utility, is sacred with both European and native.

Another bird whose habits are singular, if not

unique, is the Butcher Bird of Cape colonists (*Lanius Collaris Lin*). It is about the size of a thrush, very strongly built and with a short stout bill. When it sees a locust, a mantis, or a small bird, it pounces upon it and immediately carries it off in order to impale it on a thorn, which it does with great skill and dexterity, always passing the thorn right through the head of its victim. Every animal which it seizes is subjected to the same fate, and it continues its murderous work all day long, instigated more by love of plunder than by the desire of food. Many of its victims are left there and never even touched by it after being hung up. It never kills the creatures it catches before subjecting them to the thorn. When hungry it visits the shambles, usually an elevated branch of a tree, and picks out what seems most dainty, often examining several creatures before fixing on the one it is to eat. The Hottentots declare that it does not care for fresh food, and therefore leaves its prey on the gibbet till it becomes "high." Whatever branch or shrub is chosen by the Butcher Bird, as the place of execution, is frequently found covered with the dried carcases of singing birds, and the bodies of grasshoppers, locusts, and other insects of the larger size.

Among birds deserving of special notice are the Honey Guides which belong to the tribe of Cuckoos. These birds are regarded by both Dutch and Hottentots as infallible guides to the nests of the wild bee. They attract notice by a peculiar cry which is a sort of shrill *cher-cher*. Naturalists are not agreed regarding the truth of this peculiar instinct. Sparrman says of the Honey Guide: "I have had frequent opportunities of seeing this bird, and have been witness to the destruction of several republics of bees, by means of its treachery." On the other hand Le Valliant doubts if Sparrman ever saw the bird at all. He says that the account is "merely the repetition of a fable that is known and believed by credulous people at the Cape, and that it is false to suppose that the bird seeks to draw men after it for the purpose of sharing the plundered sweets." My experience of the Honey Guide is somewhat limited, but the following I witnessed with my own eyes. Riding one day along the edge of some sparse timber in company with a young Colonist, the shrill cry of *cher-cher* was heard, and he at once said, "There is a honey bird, let us follow it." We did so, and after hopping along from tree to tree it began to flutter over a certain spot. With little trouble we found a bees' nest which we proceeded to rob. Having removed a quantity of honeycomb, a piece was laid on an ant heap at a little distance for the bird. No sooner had my companion, who placed it there, turned his back, than down came our little friend, swift as an arrow, and proceeded to make a hearty meal with the greatest apparent relish. I think it is probable that the honey bird guides the ant bear, which does not object to honey and young bees as a variety to its white ant diet, to the nests of bees, and that the same instinct leads it to utter its *cher-cher* when men approach the places where these creatures have their stores. It is possible the same cry is uttered when any large animals happen to pass near a spot where there are colonies of bees.

From birds to butterflies is but a step, and the latter, in Africa, are among its most gorgeous products. By night and by day moths and butterflies are seen flitting about, and the most remarkable thing about them is the near resemblance borne by many varieties to the flowers on which they alight. So close is the imitation of form and colour that one, at a few paces distance, can never be sure whether he is looking at a flower simply or at the beautifully marked wings of a butterfly spread over it. Like the white ants, they have many enemies, and disguises are necessary to escape these. The most perfect disguise I have ever seen is that adopted by one species in the larval state. The creature gathers round itself bits of very slender grass stems about an inch in length. These are glued together so firmly that one cannot be separated from the bundle without destroying the whole, and so closely does this envelope resemble a thick bit of withered stem from the same grass, that one can hardly see any difference between them, even when closely examined. The ends of the tiny stems forming the sheath are so arranged as to resemble the broken end of a thick stem, and the very pith is imitated by a thin fold of tough fibrous substance with which the ends are closed. When, for the first time, my attention was called to one of these curious sheaths, I could hardly persuade myself that I had anything other than a single stem in my hand, till I had torn it open and found a large grub comfortably ensconced inside. With great difficulty a second was procured, which I kept till its occupant crept out to develop further, and then take wing to lead a new and gayer life.

There are several varieties of butterflies whose brilliant colouring is a contrast to the objects on which they rest, and who have no resemblance to leaf or flower. They float about leisurely, as if to display the beauty of their wings, or court the attack of those birds which feed so largely on winged insects. For this difference in colour-marking, the naturalist looks for some explanation. At first sight it appears as if the different varieties choose their colours in the most arbitrary manner, and that one copied nature as closely as possible, while another sought for suitable patterns in violent contrasts to nature's more sober hues. The explanation of this apparent anomaly is this :—Almost all the conspicuously coloured varieties have in their bodies acrid juices, and this is to them a sufficient protection without any mimicry of nature. For an obvious reason wasps and bees have an immunity from attack, and other insects, without offensive weapons, that resemble wasps in form and colour, share the same protection, and so the butterfly, in whose body there is no poisonous juice, has, if it bears a close resemblance to one of these varieties, the protection afforded by their obnoxious qualities. The more sober coloured butterflies have, as a rule, none of these objectionable properties, and must trust for protection to the difficulty their enemies have in seeing them. The gay-coloured species float about in the most leisurely fashion; the others dart hither and thither furtively, as if afraid of being seen, and when resting on leaf or flower hardly ever move. It is in this way nature makes compensation and keeps up the true balance among the denizens of the forest.

Another peculiarity among African insects is feigning death, and, at the same time, imitating some object. For the former one is always prepared, but, when the form is indistinguishable from surrounding objects, one is frequently taken utterly aback, and can hardly realise that he has a living creature before him. I had stopped one day for the ordinary midday meal and entered the edge of a clump of timber to look about for any new plants or insects. My groom, who accompanied me, touched me on the shoulder and said, "Has the master seen that spider before?" He, at the same time, pointed to a bush on which a number of half shrivelled, dark-brown berries hung. I looked, but there was no spider there, and was about to walk away, thinking my man was having a quiet laugh at his master's known predilection for beetles and other "varmint." But Breakfast, for such was his name, was in earnest, and, touching one of the berries, said, "It is here; this is it." The berry itself was the spider. I looked at it closely. It was just an ordinary berry, dark-brown, half shrivelled, and suspended from the twig by a stem nearly half-an-inch in length. I plucked this remarkable fruit and rolled it about in the palm of my hand. It gave no sign of life. I held it up by the stem, and still it made no complaint. I finally dropped it on the hard bare earth. It fell on its feet a spider, and the stem of the berry, having separated into six sections, showed very remarkable powers of locomotion. Unfortunately, the only specimen I had was eaten by white ants, and I am unable to give this remarkable creature's scientific name.

One variety of spiders has a most ingenious way of hiding from observation. It selects a young growing leaf, and stretches a series of cables across its under surface. As the leaf grows, its edges are kept from expanding themselves, and it forms a kind of tunnel or covered way. There the owner takes up his abode, and, without any net spread to catch the unwary, waits patiently till some insect takes shelter from a shower or for the night under the leaf, and then pounces upon it to carry it to the innermost recess of its home, and there bind it fast with strong cords. It then returns to its watch to wait the arrival of the next victim.

There is an African spider the habits of which are so unique that were the facts not already known one would hesitate to record them. It is solitary in its habits, and lives in underground chambers. Whether these are hollowed out by itself, or are the results of labours carried on by other insects I do not know. When it takes up its quarters it proceeds to fortify its home. This it does by a most ingenious contrivance. The entrance to its chamber is always vertical, and to this it fits a trap-door set on hinges of stout cable, and filling the opening with the most perfect exactness. The upper or exposed side of the door it covers over with minute pellets of earth to resemble the surrounding soil, and it finally attaches to the lower side a means of fastening down the hatch when closed. I have frequently approached one of these curious dwellings, cautiously, while open, and watched the tenant basking in the warm sunlight that poured down into his den. On making the slightest noise the door was drawn too with a snap, leaving so little appearance of life that one almost doubted the evidence of his eyes.

The Mantis comprise another tribe, which have great powers of adaptation to environment. They are found in all parts of the continent, from the brown, arid, sandy wastes, to the north of the Orange river, to the rich grassy lands of the extreme south of Kaffraria. They inhabit the rocky deserts of the Soudan, and are met with among the swamps of the Western sea-board, and they are always coloured to resemble the prevailing hues of vegetation in the district. The Mantis tribe are held in great veneration among the Hottentots, and the person on whom one happens to alight, is held in highest respect. Their habits are best observed at night. After dusk they begin to flit about, and if there is a light in a room, with an open window, they readily enter, and perch on a book or any other object they can find. There they perform that curious up-and-down motion of the head and thorax which has earned, for one South African variety, the name of *Mantis religiosa*. I never interfered with their movements when they entered my room, and can recommend them to the traveller who finds himself occupying a Kaffir hut, or camping by the edge of the forest, between the months of November and February, as very harmless and interesting companions.

Turning from insects to reptiles, we find the same adaptation of colour; and among lizards and scorpions, one has but to cross a ridge from light-coloured soil to where the ground is dark, verging on black, to find the same varieties so changed as to be scarcely recognisable. And this remarkable fact, in the case of creatures well-equipped with weapons of defence and offence, gives rise to the question of the object of such widely extending adaptation in nature. This may be restricted to colour, or it may extend to both form and colour, as in the case of the spider referred to. The former is, however, the more important.

Snakes, and poisonous reptiles of all kinds, have very peculiar skin markings, and one is, at first, at a loss to understand why some of them should be of a brilliant green, others, like the deadly puff-adder, ornamented with strange devices in various colours, a quiet yellow being conspicuous, while there are some almost entirely black. A study of their habits, and the manner in which they hunt their prey, makes it quite clear that concealment, and not warning, is the object of their skin colouring. To an animal supplied with poisonous fangs, a conspicuous colour would be a distinct advantage while on the defensive, but this advantage would be more than counterbalanced by its disadvantage while hunting for its prey. The same brilliancy of colour which would warn an enemy to keep at a safe distance, would help the object of pursuit to keep beyond the reptile's reach.

When we study snakes in their native haunts, we find that the bright-green varieties are found chiefly in the clefts of rocks where evergreen plants climb. They feed on small birds, and the close resemblance between the green foliage and the snake's skin, enables it to approach its prey unseen, or to lie still among the leaves till some unwary bird hops within its reach. Any other colouring of skin would warn the birds away. I may here remark that, from all I have ever seen, I cannot bring myself to have much faith in the so-called charming of birds by snakes. It may be true, but I have never seen it, and with the opposite, that is, birds scattering and screaming on the approach or discovery of a snake, I am quite familiar. But in nature there are so many curious phases, in different regions, and among different varieties of animals and insects, that one must always be prepared for surprises.

The Puff-adder is, again, a ground hunter. It feeds on mice, frogs, rats, moles, and other small animals. It is sluggish in its movements, and any nimble creature could keep out of its way if it were easily seen. As it lies lazily, partially covered among the decayed grass and leaves, it can hardly be distinguished from the surrounding objects by the sharpest eyes. There it patiently waits for the unsuspecting approach of rat or mole in search of its own proper food among the roots of trees or bushes. It then pounces upon its prey, and after gorging itself, will lie for days, or even weeks, as immovable as if it were a rotting branch. But, woe to the man or animal that touches it. The apparently dead adder then springs into life, and striking upwards and backwards, fixes its fangs deep into the intruder's flesh. The rest is soon told.

The black snake referred to—the Boomslang of Cape colonists, lives among the sparse mimosa timber, and preys almost exclusively on birds. The trunks and branches of mimosa trees are invariably black, and the Boomslang can climb a tree and lie on a branch unseen and unsuspected by the sharpest-eyed parrot. Only once did I see a Boomslang seize its prey. I was sitting on a stone watching the movement of a flock of brilliantly-coloured parrots. As I peered through the dense foliage of a mimosa tree, I noticed a snake creeping along one of its larger branches almost directly overhead. I began to watch its movements, and the parrots were soon forgotten. It advanced cautiously till within a foot or two of two finches perched on the branch. It then doubled its head downwards and backwards, the forward movement of the body still going on. It continued to advance in this way, but its movements were hardly perceptible, and its body was indistinguishable from the black branch on which it rested. Having advanced within reach of the birds, the point of its tail was wound round the branch, and by a movement too swift for the eye to follow, its head was thrown forward and the bird caught. It then wound itself round the branch, which was about an inch and a-half in diameter, and entangled the struggling bird in its folds. Further developments were prevented by an ounce of shot, which brought the reptile in pieces to the ground. The hour spent in watching the parrots was lost, but I had learned something.

The hooded snake (cobra de capello) is one of the most active as well as poisonous of South African reptiles. The natives dread it more than any other. It climbs into the thatch of their houses in pursuit of mice and rats, and has frequently been found coiled up among the dead embers of the fire enjoying the warmth of the hearth, or in the folds of a man's blanket. Its skin markings are very peculiar. The prevailing colour, as seen at a little distance, is a quiet green verging upon yellow or fawn colour. When examined more closely the pattern is quite distinct, and shows spots and streaks of green, brown, yellow, and drab on the back, while the colour underneath is a conspicuous light yellow. When seen in its native haunts the perfect adaptation to the prevailing tints around it is something marvellous. Its home is in the open plain, and as it lies among the grass stems, the markings of its skin so completely resemble the vegetation as to baffle the keenest eye. The green of the freshly expanded leaf, and the brown, yellow, and drab of the older and partially decayed grasses is so perfectly imitated that only by some movement does the snake betray its presence. It can in this way glide along the ground unseen and unsuspected by the creatures it is in pursuit of.

To understand the object of the bright conspicuous colour underneath, one must see a cobra on the defensive, or bidding defiance to an enemy. It then rears its head about a foot above ground, flattens out its neck and head, from which it has got the name of hooded snake, like a broad ribbon, and moving from side to side as it advances shows the bright colouring of its skin as a warning to the intruder. The cobra is a courageous reptile, and does not hesitate to show fight, and for this purpose a conspicuous skin is all important.

I once had an encounter with one in our own dining room at Duff. It was discovered under a filter stand, and it took a lot of trouble to get at it. It was not disposed to leave its shelter, but kept rearing its body and flattening out its head, while it moved slowly from side to side as if to display itself fully to view. At intervals it made a hissing noise, at the same time swelling out its neck to more than twice its normal size. It measured nearly five feet, and was a perfect specimen of its kind.

Stories illustrating the cunning and wisdom of snakes abound in Africa among both Dutch and natives. I do not attach much importance to any of them, as in the case of snakes above all other animals imagination is apt to colour the narrative. That snakes do gather and fight viciously with one another seems a well-established fact, but with what object, and in what connections such battles are fought, I have not been able to determine. I never saw such a gathering, and those who have seen them, attack the reptiles instead of waiting for further developments. I was told by a man of integrity and honour that he witnessed one such battle royal, and that snakes of different varieties fought with the greatest venom. They seemed to use their fangs, and at the same time encircle one another in their folds as is done by almost all of them to the creatures on which they prey. The assembly was attacked, and over twenty snakes killed, while a much larger number escaped into holes and crevices.

Lizards and Scorpions assume the colour of the ground and stones among which they live. If the soil is light and sandy, and the stones of a grey colour, these creatures have the same light-coloured markings. If dark, with ironstone boulders, their skins are of a tawny red or copper colour, and can hardly be distinguished, at a distance of a yard or two, from the rocks they lie upon. I have often observed their apparent security under cover of their resemblance to surrounding objects, and the general colour of the ground and rocks, and marvelled at their impudence.

There is a large class of insects whose appearance so closely resembles certain of the objects around them that it is at times difficult to obtain specimens, though one knows there are hundreds of them close at hand. Africa is a land of wonders, and one must always be prepared for fresh surprises. I had on one occasion cut out a sod of very beautiful moss, which I intended for a house plant. I was in the depth of the forest, and it was near dusk. I carried my treasure home, and only on my arrival there did I discover that I had a number of moss insects in my basket. These creatures bear so close a resemblance to the green plants they rest upon that one may pluck a sprig with an insect upon it, and only discover it is there through some slight movement on its part. To enumerate more of these peculiarities would be tedious. To understand their beauty and get thoroughly interested in them one must enter the African forest, and patiently watch every movement and sign of life. Only thus can one become acquainted with the habits of its denizens and learn something of Nature's adaptations and compensations. In the struggle for existence there is, among the lowest as among the highest forms, a certain hypocrisy practised, and though this may not quite fit in with the theory of evolution, there is in it something which harmonises with the processes of Nature, and which compels us to admit, that for its own purpose was every thing made that was made, and that for defence and assault each animal has been provided with weapons or cunning according to the requirements of its particular organisation and its mode of life.

These brief notes can hardly be said to introduce the subject to the reader, but there is here a wide field ; a field in which not much has been done, but which will amply repay the labour of the student of nature, who has the leisure and the patience to spend many days under a scorching sun on the open plains, or in the depths of the African forest. My opportunities for observation were few ; my life otherwise was too busy for that, and most of the little I was able to accomplish, was done while travelling in connection with work of a widely different nature. Often have I been interrupted in my watch of what was going on in the forest by my groom calling from a little distance, " The horses are saddled and we are ready to go." So were my birds or monkeys the moment they heard his voice, and so must we too, for the time at least, say farewell to brindled cat, spotted leopard, and tawny monkey, and leave them as well as other inhabitants of mountain and forest and plain for others, with more leisure than ever was mine, to watch their movements and tell their doings. To those who have had no opportunity of witnessing the wonders of that most wonderful of all lands, Africa, even this small contribution may be welcome.

XI.

CLIMATE AND TEMPERATURE.

THE climate of South Africa is on the whole favourable to Europeans, and the conditions of life are in most parts very pleasant. After the rains have fallen the whole face of the country is aglow with flowers and the air is laden with sweet odours. What a few weeks before presented little else than a dreary arid waste is transformed into rich pasture land and smiling meadows.

The great heat of summer is trying to some people, and a few sensitive organisations are affected with what little malaria there is, very much as people are in the centre of the continent. The temperature rises at times to 105 degrees in the shade, and when this is continued for several days life becomes almost a burden. But though the summer months are trying, there are nine months of charming weather, when week after week the same clear sky is seen, and balmy winds are experienced night and morning.

It is, in a few words, impossible to give a description that will apply to all parts of South Africa. In

Kaffraria grass lands predominate, with extensive forests at intervals. These partake of the nature of dense jungle, where creeping and climbing plants are met with in tens of thousands, and which, struggling to the tree tops for light and air, make great patches of white, red, and yellow flowers at intervals among the trees. It is in such forests the spotted leopard has his home. It is there, too, the student of nature must spend many days if he is to learn anything of the ways of its denizens. Among these shady bowers there is a profusion of life of which one has no conception on simply walking through the dense vegetation. To see what goes on one must be patient, silent, and observant. The results more than repay the labour.

In the district of the Cape Colony the most peculiar feature is the Great Karoo. This plain is about three hundred miles in length, and eighty in breadth, and forms the third terrace of Southern Africa. It is largely a parched desert, but when rain does fall the dreary waste is transformed into one continued garden of flowers. The colonist with his flocks and herds then leaves the mountains and descending into the plain, finds a wholesome and plentiful supply of food for his animals. Troops of wild ostriches, and countless herds of Antelopes come to share the spoil, and for a month or two, all revel in plenty. As the days begin to lengthen, the increased power of the sun checks the vegetation, the flowers fade and fall, the soil resumes its dry brick brown appearance. The streams dry, and the springs almost cease to flow, and by the beginning of November, the Karoo is as solitary and forsaken as it was before the rains commenced in June.

During several seasons I kept a daily record of the temperature. The highest recorded was in December, 1885, when the mercury reached 108·2 degrees in a well-shaded pavilion. The lowest was at Somerville, during the winter of 1886, at an elevation of 3500 feet above the sea level, when the thermometer recorded 7 degrees of frost.

The average maximum summer temperature at noon is about 85 degrees to 90 degrees, according to situation and elevation. The average winter temperature 60 degrees to 70 degrees, but much depends on situation and local conditions—conditions of configuration and geological formation as much as any other.

A most interesting feature of South African geology is wind markings on rocks. These are met with at many places along the coast, and if not seen in actual formation might easily be mistaken for glacier action. They are formed by the action of the wind as it blows the sand in tiny streams over the surface of the coast rocks, to form the enormous sand hills which are everywhere met with. The sand as it travels over the surface naturally follows the depressions. These are gradually worn deeper and their roughnesses smoothed down till at last long parallel grooves are formed. If, on a windy day, one of these grooves is filled up, sand begins to accumulate round the obstruction and in a very short time the groove is filled with sand, and the stream begins to flow over the obstruction. The extent of such wind markings is, in many places, considerable. About the Cape Peninsula they are found many miles inland, among corn-fields and vineyards, but where once there was a moving and shifting sea of pure white sand.

In examining such markings at the Cape, and observing their extent and variety, the question has often occurred to me, whether rock markings in other parts of the world, and more particularly the cup markings, supposed to be artificial may not have been caused by drift sand. Where there is any obstruction, or a hard pebble is embedded in the rock, the sand is diverted and swirled round and round, forming the most fantastic devices, some round, others eliptical, and many that cannot be referred to any particular form. The regularity of African winds no doubt favours their formation, but winds may have been equally regular in our latitudes in geologic time.

The visitor to the Cape who is interested in the science of Geology, will find abundance of the markings referred to along the low-lying promontories to the north of Table Bay. They may also be seen near the mouth of the Great Fish River, and to the east of the Keiskama. To seekers after health and change, the climate of Southern Africa has many attractions, and its geology and botany have much to tell. The latter especially has been largely neglected.

Then, animal life gives opportunity for study at every turn, and in this the invalid may engage with advantage.

But the typical town's-man need not go there. To him there is nothing interesting in a tangle of grass and bushes, nor are the ways of insects likely to charm in a land where insects are a pest and one of the small trials of life. The natives and their habits are to him a lot of lazy begging niggers :—This and nothing more. The country is unbearable, and its fare beastly, its means of conveyance not fit for cattle, and that just because he imagines a bit of London should follow him into the heart of the wilderness.

To the lover of nature ; the man who finds in God's own works something better and more beautiful than the false glitter of modern life, Africa will always be a land of delights and wonders, a land of romance and song ; a land with a charm which ever draws back to itself those who have tasted its bitters and its sweets, and who have been touched by its mysterious, silent, all embracing love.

www.ingramcontent.com/pod-product-compliance
Lightning Source LLC
Chambersburg PA
CBHW031957230426
43672CB00010B/2189